Adventures of a
Vintage Car
Collector

"The New Life of the Old Turnpike," 1907, by George S. Dubuis *(Courtesy David David, Inc., Philadelphia, Pa.)*

Adventures of a

Vintage Car Collector

By ALAN L. RADCLIFF

with Postscripts by Barbara B. Radcliff

E. A. SEEMANN PUBLISHING, INC.

Miami, Florida

Copyright © 1972 by Alan L. Radcliff

Library of Congress Catalog Card No. 72-82923

ISBN 0-912458-18-6

Manufactured in the United States of America

To my wife Barbara
for her limitless humor, patience and help over the years,

and to our friend

Arthur Delman, for his devotion to our
cars, and to us.

Contents

Illustrations

(Full color illustrations in italics)

Foreword

A BRIEF HISTORY OF THE AUTOMOBILE

Before 1900, the automobile was in healthy gestation, and its sudden unheralded birth was accompanied by loud yells and a good slap on the behind. A giant had been born, but to start with it looked about the same size as any other baby.

None of the designer-godfathers of that time was sure whether the baby should be rolled on three or four wheels, or even what the wheels should be made of; no one was sure of anything. But the baby was a strong, husky kid, and no illness or accident kept him down very long.

Despite the fact that there was a good deal of experimental work in the nineties, and though Alexander Winton built a horseless carriage in 1895, it wasn't until Henry Ford came along later with his production internal-combustion engine of a simplified design that things really started moving. Matters were mostly confused. The bounty race for a practical, economical, trustworthy concept was still scattered about in the early 1900s among steam, electric, and gasoline vehicles, with each inventor claiming his approach to be the best. This was naturally to be expected, but the final decision was going to be made by the customer, not the inventor.

By 1903 the "industry" had started to expand when the Brecht Automobile Company of Saint Louis tried to solve all the problems at once by embracing all the extant possibilities. They announced an erector set package, where the purchaser could make his own choice about assembling his own car, electric, steam or gas. Since the average price of a horseless buggy in those days was about $700 (Fords were about $450) the knock-down, do-it-yourself offer looked like a winner, at lower cost. Obviously this foolishness couldn't go on. In rapid succession, the Knox, the Haynes, the Trumbull, the Oldsmobile, the Reo, the Cadillac, the Pierce, the Stoddard-Dayton, and a host of others crowded in on the expanding market. In England a great name appeared on the motorcar scene. Rolls Royce announced in 1907 that its "Silent Six" touring car was available at $8,000, a staggering figure for those days when $1,000 was a small fortune and a nickel bought a quart of milk.

In the 35 years between that bustling era and the Second World War, the gasoline engine development was swift, sure, and invincible. Hundreds of new brands sprang up like weeds in the United States and Europe. It seemed that virtually every buggy maker and bicycle maker, every railroad engineer and aircraft designer, even general mechanics and village blacksmiths tried their luck in this tremendous bonanza. This was all to the good. Ideas from here and there and everywhere began to coalesce into what was soon to become the greatest organized industrial effort in the history of mankind.

Steering designs were as variegated as engine power experiments. In leading up to the steering wheel, the range of devices was bewildering. The earliest, boat type tillers changed position from left side to right side, to middle, and then to foot-operated controls that must have been frightening to manage. Drivers steered from the front seat and from the rear seat, and passengers had to take their chances. Noisy and menacing driving mechanisms were offered in endless varieties, from chain drives to double chain drives, rear end drives, and front end drives. It was a time of ebullient experimentation, and everyone was having a ball.

The thinning-out process began with the steam car. Having been the natural outgrowth of the earlier steam engine, it was the first to fall out of ranks because of its unwieldiness and inconveniences. Imagine being out in the plains with no rivers or streams about, and running out of *water!* (Of course this could happen just as easily in those days with gas, but somehow the psychology about "water" created a different kind of carelessness.) In a procession of failures, some spectacular, some unnoticed, the inadequate designs were rapidly eliminated from the aggressive battle, and attrition took its natural course. The emergence of the successful companies of that era paralleled their ability to offer constant improvement, increases in speed, durability, and better appearance.

A new sense of achievement and recognition of greater opportunities led the designers of the day to search out more efficient accessories for safe and comfortable driving; even the inevitable luxuries began to appear on certain higher-priced models. But the basics were what counted most to the average buyer, and greater concentration was devoted to such items as smoother gears, better headlights, surer brakes, sweeter horns, stronger wheels and tires. Instruments and simpler engine controls were a great sales feature, and suddenly front doors began to appear as body styles developed smartly after 1910. In 1912 the newest rage was the electric starter, which literally revolutionized the world of the automobile; now a woman or even the senior citizen could drive a gasoline car without having to crank the engine! The next evolutionary phase weighed this interesting factor into balance, and some forward-looking designers began to think of their cars in light of the potential women's market. Though this was still more than a decade away in terms of mass or significance, it was never too early to look ahead.

Drivers appeared out of the woodwork. Anyone who knew how to run a horse and buggy appeared in goggles and dusters, and race clubs began to spring up around the countryside. By 1912 international driving competition began to flourish. The craze was universal. Racing became the new and fashionable Gentlemen's Sport.

In Europe, well aware of the revolution that was taking place in the world of personal transportation, a coterie of famous designers of aircraft engines pushed their way into the field. It would have been difficult to keep them out; they had great contributions to make to the automobile engine. In applying their special knowledge to earthbound propulsion, they quickly and inexorably established themselves as the leaders and the geniuses in mechanical refinements, and became the masters of the European race circuits. The great names, the legendary names, began to shine out from the dim recesses of their workrooms and drafting tables: W. O. Bentley of England, Mark Birkight of Sweden with his French built Hispano-Suiza, Ferdinand Porsche who joined Mercedes-Benz in 1923, Ettore Bugatti, the inimitable Italian. All these and many more illustrious designers all over Europe fashioned and constructed the most magnificent machines of all time. Any one of their creations today is a collector's prize, sought after, auctioned like a great painting, paid for at incredible prices, and cherished like crown jewels.

From the power plant emphasis of the early twenties, the shift toward beauty and grace in body styling became quite demanding, as the realization grew that sheet metal could be wielded into any shape and that, like sculpture, it was capable of three-dimensional elegance and excitement. The market was there, and the money flowed freely. Exotic tastes in the world of high fashion, and the dynamic social stepladder forced the sudden debut of numerous custom coachbuilders in England, France, Germany, and Italy. The Americans, not to be outdone on any level in those early days, also clamored for their share of the fabulous new "special coachwork" windfall. But it was to be many years before they caught up to their European counterparts.

Of the great and famous marques mentioned previously, all enjoyed the prestige of "one-off" (one-of-a-kind) bodies; this in itself was a very rarified form of snobbery. The wealthier the client, presumably the more unique the body design, all within the confines, of course, of the ability of the client to understand what the designer was after.

Standing alone, through the years of default and weeding out of the ranks, is the incredibly durable and always exquisite Rolls Royce, unquestionably the world's greatest marque for precision quality, craftsmanship, longevity of use, beauty of design, variety, and consistent, secured value. In prestige it is unequalled by any other car except perhaps for the vaunted Duesenberg. On the whole, it may be safely asserted that there has never been any other motorcar to contest the continuous success and rarified position of the singularly eminent Rolls Royce. The cars associated with this grand name have always been conceived as far more than objects of usefulness, and paradoxically this very usefulness has endured beyond the imagination of designers who laid emphasis on beauty and glamour alone. The first car to bear the proud name is reported to be in superb condition today, and though it is a unique museum piece, it undoubtedly will start up at a few swings of the crank handle. A published statement to that effect may still be found. "The life of a Rolls Royce motorcar which has been properly treated is almost indefinite." More special bodies have been mounted on these indestructible chassis, by more custom coachbuilders, than all of the other famous ultra-priced motorcars combined.

In the heydey years before the 1929 crash, astronomical prices were no deterrent. Individuality and snobbery created their own price levels, and the cost be damned. Fabulous cars were built in prices ranging from $15,000 to $35,000. Indian maharajahs were famed for their largesse in ordering cars with brocaded and petitpoint interiors. They featured built-in liquor bars with inlaid cabinetry, writing desks that folded into the seat divider, and other fanciful compartments tailored to personal desires, and aimed only at the gratification of their owners. Several Rolls Royces were made in those years for European royalty with hand painted panels, by famous artists, installed into the sidewalls and ceilings of the passenger section.

With all this froufrou going on in Europe, it was inevitable that at least one American automobile would aspire to such heights on this side of the Atlantic. The most famous and sought-after motorcar, ascending to its own peak reputation in the late twenties and early thirties, was the unimpeachable Duesenberg, often mistaken by the uninitiated for a German marque. This gorgeous, yet overbearing, huge car was built in Indianapolis, Indiana, U.S.A., within a stone's throw of the famous "Indy Speedway." Back in 1928 our country had already proved it had the technical and design ability to produce one of the very great cars of all time. The Duesenberg became the fabled choice and ultimate status symbol for the world's millionaires. Princes, tycoons of industry, Hollywood personalities, and the great sportsmen of both continents waited in line for their turn to own one, at prices between $12,500 and $25,000. With extra-fancy bodywork, a special "Dussey" could even go beyond that figure. But the buyers got their money's worth. Styling equalled or surpassed the leading European luxury cars, but the happy owner also got the power, excitement, and speed of a racing machine with the huge and imperial straight-eight Duesenberg engine. Some models, supercharged in the early thirties, were capable of over 100 mph in second gear, and offered a top speed of up to 130 mph! Fred Duesenberg, its designer, and the Lycoming factory where these superb engines were built, certainly knew what they were doing, and had proved it on the racing track for many years. The SJ (supercharged) engine with its gleaming chrome side exhausts, was reputed to rev up to 320 horsepower when you floored the accelerator (if you dared).

It was therefore natural that the greatest coachbuilders in the world wanted to get their body designs onto these frighteningly magnificent chassis. Some of their most beautiful bodies were designed right in the Duesenberg plant by Chief Designer Gordon Buehrig, or his successor J. Herbert Newport. Many were built by LeGrande, a company also owned by Duesenberg. A number of the great coachbuilders in America who had weathered the depression years, including Le Baron, Judkins, Murphy, Locke, and others, vied for the privilege and distinction of working with the world's bigshots, designing breathtaking bodies that seemed to stretch out a mile long.

It is interesting to imagine that you are a prospective owner of one of these masterpieces in, say 1931, and have chosen Murphy to build the body in his California works. Picture, if you will, meeting with a staff of designers, engineers, and stylists in a big conference room, with a mysterious huge blackboard down at one end of the room. You have an animated conversation in which you express, to your best layman's ability, the personal dreams you have had about your own special Duesenberg. You have seen others, perhaps been driven in them, and your mind is swirling with images and flashes of fender shapes, sidemount wheels, body types, interior fittings and decoration, slanting windshields, and sweeping profiles and configurations. As you describe your thoughts, rough sketches are being swiftly put to paper and instantly revised as you mull over some vague detail in your ideas. The discussion continues, and suddenly you are looking at an incomplete, yet recognizable, stylist's rendering of what you have been struggling to explain. It may not be perfect, it may not be exactly what you've glimpsed in your mind, but it's close enough to give you a satisfying thrill that your desire will be translated to metal, leather, and glass. In a few days or a few weeks, depending on the current schedule at Murphy's, you will be presented with a sheaf of color renderings to choose from. You may combine elements from any drawing with any other (within reason) until the happy compromise is reached with the designers.

A short time later you will find yourself in the big conference room again, and see that your final choice has been transferred to the huge blackboard at the end of the room in full size and in almost perfect detail! You'll stand back, secretly jubilant, suggest some final alterations, ask politely for opinions, and approve construction. From then on you're out of it for awhile, as the chassis has to be shipped in from Indianapolis, built to the specific wheelbase needed for your particular design. You'll be called upon several months later, perhaps, to decide about materials, textures, final colors, and other options available before the car is finished to its minutest details. Then you'll ecstatically drive it away one rare day, and know that you had a deeply personal part in its creation. That may be one of the secret weapons they gave you to begin with. All you needed was some patience—and the money.

This ceremonious making of a Duesenberg was by no means the standard treatment. It was a feature of the Murphy organization, though undoubtedly offered in some lesser form, possibly without the big blackboard panoply, by other *carossiers* of the period. Quite often too, a Duesenberg chassis would be shipped to Europe for the more daring designs of the Continental coachbuilders. Obviously, it would not be as easy for the future American owner to stay involved with his car on a step-by-step basis, considering the lengthy ocean-liner crossings in those days, unless of course he chose to stay in France or Italy while the car was being constructed. That was one of the advantages the European customer *could* enjoy.

In today's world of antique and classic car collectors, the highest prize one can hope for is to own one of these almost stupendous automobiles which went out of production in 1936 because of a series of strange and heart-breaking events in management, and growing competition from the rather expensive but comparatively lower-priced luxury cars such as Packard, Cadillac, Lincoln, and Pierce-Arrow. Current prices on classic Duesenbergs, not even restored to peak condition, are about two and a half times the original cost, and at an auction in 1971, a bid of $68,000 was turned down by the owner for a near-perfect touring phaeton. It is anticipated by many experts in the field that within three years some great "Duesey" will sell beyond the six-figure mark.

The "Golden Classic Era," that period from 1925 to 1941, right up to World War II, left us with a great heritage, an array of beautiful and glamorous motorcars that have rightly taken their place within the world's established and recognized arts. The happy result of this growing "magnificent obsession" is the restoration of many hundreds of thousands of vintage automobiles, from Fords to Rolls Royces to Duesenbergs, that have been retrieved from abandoned garages, junkyards, piled-up barns, and even caves where they were left by some perceptive persons, then forgotten—rotting away during the depression years. Many great engines have been found in wheat fields and on ships, where they served a tour of duty as farm implements or boat winches! Those fortunate enough to have discovered "basket cases" in the late forties, fifties, and early sixties are way ahead of the game. Many collectors also had the good fortune to find great automobiles in good running condition on used car lots, where only "cosmetics" were required for prize-winning restorations and huge increases in value.

The growth of this hobby has been phenomenal since 1960. Collectors around the world proudly exhibit their rare motorcars to the public in regular Concours d'Elegance meets. Many clubs abound in the United States and Europe, led by the austere Antique Automobile Club of America (AACA). Together with the Classic Car Club of America (CCCA), they list multitudes of collectors in their thick directories. Individual marques of almost every type manufactured also have their own private clubs such as the Rolls Royce Owners Club (RROC), Bentley Drivers' Club, "ACD" Club

(Auburn, Cord, Duesenberg), and perhaps the largest of all, the Old Ford Club.

The major purpose of these clubs is to foster the restoration and competition-judging of their jewels of the past. The winning of a $4 trophy often represents thousands of dollars in restoration costs alone (it can cost up to $15,000 to restore a great, rare automobile) plus the hundreds of painstaking owner-hours of concentrated effort, supervision, hopes, and dreams.

This is the Name of The Game. Come join the fun!

Adventures of a

Vintage Car
Collector

Prologue

As a young boy, as early as the age of nine, I was already able to discern, from a good distance, the outline and configuration of almost any model of automobile on the streets of New York. One of my favorite games was to call out to anyone present the name, year, and body style while a car was still several blocks away. Walks along Park Avenue filled me with awe, as I spotted great cars parked along the curb, guarded by their uniformed chauffeurs. As I became older and more proficient in this heady sport, I found more exotic challenges via the advertisements in popular magazines of the day. This was a breathtaking exposure to the rare and mighty automobiles of the Classic Era, in the early thirties. By some natural process of absorption, the lines and shape of any vehicle automatically became engraved in my memory bank (to live again another day). Little did I know then what this youthful affair was to lead me into in later life.

My boundless zest for this creative personal expression increased rather than abated as the years went on. Most particularly, my father suffered through tense conflicts with me each time a change of family cars was being planned. I would canvass the local automobile dealers on my bicycle, accumulating a dazzling, colorful welter of brochures for his inspection, to the point where the poor man became totally bewildered with the endless choices of Buicks, Chryslers, Studebakers, Packards, Cadillacs, Lincolns. But somehow we never went beyond Buicks and Chryslers. I could never understand this in my youth.

My college years floated away amid a passing parade of flashy "rich boy's" convertibles, while the best I could boast was a simple Ford or Chevy coupe—in every case, however, with some special individuality added, either striping, two-toning, or a special hood ornament. After the war, in rapid succession (during my early career on Madison Avenue) I owned a new '46 Ford convertible, a new '48 Mercury convertible, a new '50 Buick convertible, and then a regal, expensive new 1952 green-and-yellow Daimler convertible. The latter was enticingly sold to me as being the same colors as one then owned by Princess Margaret, though I never *really* had the opportunity to check this out personally.

During those years as I gadded about as a bachelor it was quite a jolt to see some of the greatest classic cars rotting away in junkyards all over the countryside, or standing orphaned and unwanted in used car lots. I used to stop and stare with sharp desire and compassion at the lost glory of these behemoths, the monstrous Duesenbergs, big Packard phaetons and roadsters, Cadillac V-16s, and even an occasional exquisite Rolls Royce. In the early fifties it was not uncommon to find a lineup of Duesenbergs on a Manhattan used car lot selling for $500 to $1,000 each (today's price $35,000-$75,000), many of them in quite decorous condition. Looking backward from my swivel chair, I often brood about the forever lost opportunities; $800 for a "Duesey" phaeton? $600 for a Rolls Royce roadster? And yet like many of my then unintuitive collector-cohorts who now kick themselves to kingdom-come with vengeance, I never had the guts to buy one of these incredible prizes, while asininely wasting many thousands of dollars instead on chromy new "Detroit Iron" vehicles that became obsolete in two or three years. Such hindsight from the running board!

In the years that followed, I went through some fine beauties, including a 1954 XK-120 Jaguar convertible, and later, the pinnacle American sports car of its day (which I purchased right off the floor at the International Auto Show at the New York Coliseum), the renowned 1956 Packard-Studebaker "Golden Hawk." This was the car that went with me when I "recycled" my life to Florida in 1956, and it was here that I met and married my adorable and fun-loving wife Barbara ("Bobbie").

One of our earliest moments of rapport occurred when I learned that her father had been a crackerjack automobile dealer in Boston, and that she had also grown up in an atmosphere of "wheels-and-deals." This similar background conspired and helped to bring us together, so we could pursue the Mad Automobile Caper, which was threaded prominently through our lives, but always parallel to my successful new manufacturing venture in Florida. Then came our boys Jonathan and Bennett, and all of the other goodies that make life rewarding and stimulating: foreign travel, home-building, art collecting, sailing, civic work, friends, and goals realized.

We didn't know it then, but the best was yet to come—that gladiator's arena of the antique and vintage cars. Of all the personal endeavors we have ever known, no other has come near the joys and thrills of car collecting.

1

Days of Wine and Hoses

We were first sharply bitten by the paralyzing vintage-car bug in 1962, during our first trip to Europe. In London, it was astonishing to see countless cars of the thirties and older, in daily use. Automobiles thirty to forty years "young" are cherished possessions; the British do not allow vanity to supersede practicality. Paint, leather, and chrome may be slightly "tatty," but engines and mechanical details are kept at peak function. They regard American vintage car collectors as slightly neurotic since their own standards of restoration end with "nice" appearance, while emphasizing mechanical perfection. We have attended several antique car shows in England—always quite a shock to an American car restorer. In my opinion, some of the nice prize-winning cars there couldn't score 75 points in our basic 100 point system in the United States. That's not even Third Place.

We found ourselves yearning for a good "$1,000 example" to take home to Florida. Research yielded the names of several vintage car dealers in London, and we started making the rounds. Being neophytes in the game, we were amazed and disillusioned to learn that $1,000 didn't create much seller enthusiasm.

We looked at several aged Rolls Royces, the baggiest of them starting at about $3,000; a couple of run-down Lagondas and Bentleys at about $2,000; raunchy Rileys, and battered Jaguars at over $1,200. Obviously some adjustments had to be made in our gunsights, as $1,000 brought us down to a "heap" or the tiny vintage MG level! Being a 6'2", 200 pounder, this possibility was quickly abandoned, and we certainly were not interested in a pile of trouble.

We realized, too, that imports had to be calculated at starting cost, plus freight, insurance, taxes, U.S. Customs, and all the unknowns of restoring to show-competition levels. How much was that? We decided to wait until we got back to the States, to learn a little more about the "true" value of cars, the restoration art, and so on. (Looking back ruefully, after importing four cars from Britain in the ensuing years, we certainly let some fantastic bargains slip away back in 1962!)

Around that same time we were deep in the bog of designing our new house on the bay in Coconut Grove, a two-year architectural planning project. We decided reluctantly that under the circumstances we didn't have time (or spare cash) to heed the suppressed car yearning. But the next summer, while on a vacation trip to New York, our resolve was smashed when we made a point of visiting the Vintage Car Store in Nyack. This was a new "emporium," one of the first special retailers in the country offering a tantalizing variety of antique and classic cars and leading in the real galloping collectors' craze that was obviously developing. The selection was, by today's standards, quite epicurean. A gleaming Duesenberg was on display at $9,000 (1972 price tag $60,000), a Rolls Royce roadster, in excellent condition, at $5,500. Packard, Lincoln, and Pierce-Arrow touring phaetons were offered at about $6,000. A tired but glamorous Mercedes-Benz 540 K was $5,000, a National First Prize Boattail Auburn Speedster was $4,600. (These cars are now double, triple, and even four times these prices.)

We fell in love at first sight with a sleek 1936 British Alvis 4.3 liter roadster. It was a certified "One-Off," with an all-aluminum body, price $3,000. Not yet being oriented to the fact that famous "name brands" were the coming thing, we mulled it over, easily convinced each other by nightfall, and returning the next day offered $2,600 which was accepted, somewhat to our surprise and consternation. With assurances from the store that all details of shipment to Florida would be carefully handled, C.O.D., we left for home congratulating ourselves on a shrewd buy.

A couple of weeks slipped by, with no further acknowledgment. Getting worried, we phoned the store. Our freshman education about vintage car collecting was about to begin.

"There have been some problems about finding a transporter to pick up the Alvis in Nyack, but we're working on it," I was told. "Be patient."

I promised to be patient. Another fruitless week went by, another long-distance phone call was made.

"No luck," we were told. "Even if we deliver the car to New York City, we haven't found anyone to bring it down to Florida."

The 1936 4.3 liter Alvis in front of the author's office.

There sat our splendid Alvis in Nyack. Should I fly up and try to drive it back? No, it was too risky to expect the sleek old girl to make the 1,500 mile trip. Were there any Miami transporters to go up and bring her back? None to be found here either. How about sea freight from a New Jersey port? There was no such service available. About eleven desperate phone calls later, the only possible solution grievously presented itself. Riddle Airlines was willing to take it from Newark Airport to Miami for a "nominal" charge of $760!

Realizing with anguish that this was now a no-choice situation, we made our final phone call to the store. Yes, they would arrange to truck it to Newark for $65, but we got no sympathy for our inherited pains. Three days later, feverish and jumpy after losing contact completely with the expedition, we suddenly received notice from the airline that the Alvis had landed at Miami.

I rushed out to the airport, arriving as our two-ton monster was craned out of the huge cargo door and gently set to rest on the ground with a small bump.

In gratitude for our exceptional efforts, our beauty refused to start up. Two hours later, after much guesswork, tinkering, frustration, and repeated pushing, the light of our lives cranked up, sputtered, and ran. Driving her home was a palpitating event unequaled in our memory.

There she finally crouched in our garage, sneering, we thought, at the temerity of Americans who want to own an aged British car, circa 1936.

The next step in the learning process was to join a local club for fun-and-games. The elusive Vintage Car Club of Miami's phone number was eventually discovered, and Charlie Sebastian, the club director, greeted us warmly. The next Sunday we proudly joined the ranks at a park outing, and beamingly accepted the plaudits of the membership. Vintage European cars were not too common in Florida at the time.

This was the opening foray in what was to become the most arduous and continuous personal commitment of our lives, but we were dumb, blind, and happy!

POSTSCRIPTS BY MY WIFE

It all seemed to take hold so innocently, coming into our lives softly like a sweet, enveloping, summertime London fog. At first it was just a helter-skelter, spicy interest in early model cars. Who could guess that the bug-bite would send our fever soaring to 105 degrees?

When Alan first started dancing his tricky gavotte with all those "old" cars in England, I was mildly amused—and a little curious too. I said to myself (I often talk to myself, best consultant I know), "Let him have a good time, what harm can it do?" Famous last words.

Then on that fate-written trip to New York and Nyack, where we got hooked, but good, on the Alvis, I said to myself reasonably, "Look, he's a good man. He's worked hard, and things are beginning to go right. We have two healthy boys, and everyone's happy. So if he wants a new toy, he certainly deserves it. It won't bother me. I like cars too!"

That's how nonchalantly treaties are made, and wars lost.

Each one of our cars had individual personalities, and therefore to me, names were required. The Alvis was "Black Beauty," out of my childhood memories.

She crouched in the carport, long, black, and lean, ready to rear back on her spoke wheels and fly off when Alan placed his loving hands on her steering wheel. She had a deep throaty roar that burbled down her exhaust, while her engine purred like a sleek panther.

I remember one of Alan's great pleasures was to take her up on the expressway and "blow her out." This usually began by a warming-up period of say 45 mph at 3,000 rpm. At this point some curious male driver would ride abreast asking, "What kind of car is that? What year?" and always with tongue in cheek, "Want to drag?"

Alan would nod, downshift his loved one, and stomp the gas pedal to the floor. Black Beauty would plunge forward in a gray cloud of exhaust smoke, reaching 90 mph before the stupefied driver could close his mouth.

She was really a magnificent beast. I loved her too for her captivating personality and curvaceous lines. And I won my spurs also, in right-hand driving, in the Alvis.

B.B.R.

1936 4.3 liter Alvis Roadster after restoration

1924 3 liter Red Label Bentley Tourer by Van Den Plas

2

So Much to Learn

 Weeks of energetic work and diligent planning followed in preparation for *Our First Show,* to be held at a Fort Lauderdale park. Advice poured in from well-wishers, neighbors, club members, even our kids. Everyone polished, touched up paint, washed canvas and carpets, tinkered with the engine, and tightened nuts and bolts. It was a community love affair.

The great day arrived. Bobbie wondered naively, "Will we take First Prize?"

"Why not," I said proudly, neophyte restorer that I was. "She's a beauty, look at those gorgeous lines! "

We drove into the show grounds and lined up between a leather-bodied '29 Bentley tourer and a '30 Packard roadster, both magnificently restored after years of costly rebuilding and fine detailing. How *much* we had to learn about competition points and first prize perfection was obvious as we gazed with awe at our glittering neighbors.

That night at the awards banquet, ingenuously still hoping, we gulped dinner, and with hearts pounding awaited the announcements. Ah, our class 19-B was now being called. Third prize was awarded—no, not us! Could we be second prize? No, again! Good Lord, are we first?

Our sweet Alvis was passed over without even a word of comment. We were stunned, mystified, and chagrined. Nothing it seemed, had ever mattered so much. Education of the gullible is slow and painful.

A major reassessment took place throughout the next few weeks. In all fairness, we now realized that trophy winners were rare and difficult to create; competition is fierce and unyielding in the American point system.

We had to accept, somewhat sadly, that the winning cars *were* relatively flawless, and that beauty and distinctive body design *were not* the standards for judging. We now knew that detailing and authenticity were what counted most, and that the most ordinary Model T Ford, excellently restored, could beat the fenders off the most glamorous Rolls Royce with pitted chrome or cracked leather.

We learned gradually that this entire mad business of the antique car shows is mainly successful because of the innate competitiveness in the human spirit (at least we have always firmly believed that to be true), and that gave us a decided edge, as we two have no shortage of this natural commodity! Aside from the extraordinary preparations and apprehensions that go with the restoration and exhibiting of cars, it really takes a couple of years of experience and perspiration to fully understand the subtle differences between "Local," "Regional," and "National" meets.

The French coined a phrase, "Concours d'Elegance," to describe the stateliness of exhibiting automobiles, which seems like a slight overstatement to describe a bunch of beautiful old cars, sometimes leaking grease and rusty water, lined up on a lawn in a public park or in a steamy shopping center parking lot. But the elegance comes from the cars *themselves,* and not the surroundings. True, it would be grand to have our antique car meets in the courtyard of Versailles Palace, or in the Place de la Concorde in Paris, but since this is not possible, we have learned to paint in the background with the loving brush strokes of our imagination. And, now and then, we do manage to arrange a local show at a glamorous spot like Viscaya in Miami, and then the "Concours" is for real.

The Local shows served up by the smaller independent clubs usually attract between 50 and 100 cars from nearby areas. There are three or four of these delightful small meets a year in Florida. The majority of the car clubs these days are affiliated with the national organizations such as the Antique Automobile Club of America (AACA), the Classic Car Club of America (CCCA), the Rolls Royce Owners Club (RROC), the Old Ford Club, and so on. Shows by these clubs are of a wider regional nature; collectors from all over the state and nearby states drive or trailer their beauties long distances for the event. There is even a trophy for "The Car Driven the Longest Distance." Car registration for the more important of these meets can total up to 300, and the show grounds must necessarily be large enough to accommodate the cars, their owners and guests, plus as many as 20,000 visitors during the one or two days of the meet.

Most cities graciously offer their public parks free for these occasions and assist with publicity, groundskeepers, guards, and rest facilities. Admission is generally free to the public, and the only costs to the awed visitor are his hotdogs and colas, or a trinket purchased from a stand in the ubiquitous "flea market" where one may find a headlight from the 1910 era, tires from milk delivery trucks of the 1920s, front springs from an old Packard, rusty hubcaps and wheels, and now and then, the hood ornament from a vintage Rolls Royce (but *that* takes luck).

The National meet is another matter entirely. Since our nation is so spread out that driving to a California show might be out of the question, there are six to eight separate meets a year operating under the same rules, in the AACA for example. The choosing of the Regional chapters to run these meets in different parts of the country is a rare privilege that must be won "on the merits" by any specific Region. The competition for this signal honor begins years before the final selections are made, and the glamorous title of "National Meet, Southeastern Division," for instance, is awarded to the most active club in the entire region, the main considerations being based upon the accomplishments, reputation, facilities, management, and "charisma" of the specific chapter. This is quite a race in itself! Our Fort Lauderdale AACA Region has had the distinction of garnering two "Nationals" in the past five years, a source of great pride to its members.

Judging standards vary with the importance of the event. The comparatively simple 100-point system (none of it is really simple) is still in use for smaller shows, but the larger Regionals, and of course the Nationals, operate under a fairly new 1,000-point system, which simply means to the groaning car restorer that he can be "cut into finer ribbons by relative tenths of a point" rather than by the point or half-point. A National First Prize car must score over 950 points to win the coveted, ultimate award, which is a small, oval, enameled metal plaque that must be affixed to the car forever, stating: "National First Prize Winner." If no car in any class attains this minimum score, there is no first prize in that class.

Judging, at any car show, by trained panels of experts, is a hairy matter (I have had the pleasure of working in the blasting sun for three hours straight as a judge at many shows myself), as one may constantly see himself mirrored in the anxious owner's eyes, aware that only a short time later the judge becomes the *judged,* if he happens to have a car of his own at the meet! A 1,000 point AACA score sheet is reproduced herewith, and it will, I expect, strike fear into the heart of the reader, very much as it does to the collector-exhibitor.

The granddaddy of all antique car shows, the annual culmination

ANTIQUE AUTOMOBILE CLUB OF AMERICA

Judging Form, revised January 1970

NOTE: (NA) DENOTES NON-AUTHENTIC, OR MISSING COMPONENT, TAKE MAX. DEDUCTION EXCEPT AS NOTED.

GROUP 1 EXTERIOR AND UNDERSIDE FINISH: Body, fenders, running boards, splash aprons, hard top, wheels and chassis.   (TOTAL DEDUCTIONS)

*Metallic (NA)	—15	Rust-chipping	—1 —5 —10	Straightness	—1 —5 —10	(NA) Matl. incl. body,	
Wrong Color	—1 —10 —20	Peeling and		Fender beads	—1 —5 —10	fenders, etc. —10 —20 —30	
Luster	—1 —5 —10	scratches	—1 —5 —10	Welting	—1 —5 —10	Wrong body	—50
Orange peel	—1 —5 —10	Pits	—1 —5 —10	Undercoating	—10		
Runs	—1 —5 —10	Dents	—1 —5 —10	Striping	—1 —5 —10		
OTHERS:							

NOTE: Metallic paint available after Nov. 1, 1927, if used owner must prove.

GROUP 2 CHASSIS, WHEELS, TIRES: Excluding paint and plating.   (TOTAL DEDUCTIONS)

Repairs (NA)	—1 —5 —10	Tires and wheels—		Rear axle	—1 —5 —10	Lube fitting	—1 —5 —10
Steering	—1 —3 —5	rims		Trans. Dr. Line	—1 —5 —10	Lack of lube	—1 —3 —5
(power) (NA)	—10	(—1 —3 —5 ea. max.—20‡)		Shocks	—1 —5 —10	Excess lube	—1 —3 —5
Front axle	—1 —5 —10	Fabric tire cover	—1 —3 —5	Gas tank	—1 —3 —5	Muffler—pipes	—1 —5 —10
Brakes (NA)	—10	Springs (NA)	—1 —5 —10	Body bolts (NA)	—1 —5 —10	Fuel supply device see group 5	
OTHERS:							

‡NOTE: Max. ded. —20 (demountable-non-demountable (NA) —5 ea. Incorrect size if available —5 ea.)
(mismatched or badly worn —5 ea. good pairs O.K.)

GROUP 3 BRIGHT WORK: Condition and alignment, excluding interior and engine compartment.   (TOTAL DEDUCTIONS)
Incorrect plating, % absence of correct plating or paint. 1% to 5% —1, to 25% —5, to 50% —10, to 100% —20.

Bumpers	—1 —5 —10	*Head lights	—1 —5 —10	*Gas gen.	—1 —5 —10	Lock rings (rim)	—1 —5 —10
Rad shell	—1 —5 —10	*Side lights	—1 —5 —10	*Prestolite tank	—1 —3 —5	Hub caps	—1 —5 —10
Rad grill	—1 —5 —10	*Tail lights	—1 —3 —5	Mirrors, ext.	—1 —3 —5	Stem covers	—1 —3 —5
Rad orn.	—1 —3 —5	*Driving lights	—1 —5 —10	Windshield	—1 —5 —10	Metl. tire cover	—1 —3 —5
Rad core see Grp. 5		Horn, ext.	—1 —3 —5	Door handles	—1 —3 —5	Trim	—1 —3 —5
OTHERS:							

NOTE: Incorrect lights —5 —10, sealed beams (NA) — 10 per pair. Max. ded. — 35 all lights (NA)

GROUP 4 INTERIOR: Condition and alignment, upholstery, soft-hard top, interior brightwork and paint.   (TOTAL DEDUCTIONS)
(NA) Top matl. —5 —10 —15   (NA) Upholstery matl. —1 —15 —30   (NA) Interior plating —1 —3 —5

Top down	—20	*Side curtains	—1 —3 —5	Heel board	—1 —3 —5	Hardware	—1 —5 —10
‡Top-trim	—1 —5 —10	§Seats	—1 —5 —10	Windwiper	—1 —3 —5	Steer. wheel	—1 —3 —5
note #—40)	—40	§Seat backs	—1 —5 —10	Glass	—1 —5 —10	Pedals—levers	—1 —3 —5
Top iron-bow	—1 —5 —10	§Side panels	—1 —5 —10	Rear window (NA)	—1 —3 —5	Dash & inst.	—1 —3 —5
Head lining	—1 —5 —10	Floor cover	—1 —5 —10	Door molding	—1 —3 —5		
OTHERS:							

NOTE: ‡Top missing —40 (if iron and fitted). #Top style (NA) —10.
*Side curtains (NA) or missing if car equipped for same —5.
§Upholstery style (NA) max. ded. —20 all items. Trim max. ded. —5.

GROUP 5 ENGINE COMPARTMENT: Condition and alignment, including paint and brightwork.   (TOTAL DEDUCTIONS)

Plating	—1 —5 —10	Carburetor	—1 —5 —10	*Starter	—1 —5 —10	Splash pans	—1 —3 —5
*Block—head	—1 —5 —10 —50	Magneto-Dist	—1 —5 —10	Generator	—1 —3 —5	Wiring	—1 —3 —5
Crankcase	—1 —3 —5	Coil	—1 —3 —5	Fan belts	—1 —3 —5	Terminals	—1 —3 —5
Excess oil	—1 —3 —5	Priming cups	—1 —3 —5	Horn, int.	—1 —3 —5	Tape	—1 —3 —5
Manifolds	—1 —3 —5	Water pump	—1 —3 —5	*Fuel supply device	—1 —5 —10	Tubing	—1 —3 —5
*Rad core	—1 —5 —10 —20	Hose clamps	—1 —5 —10	Firewall	—1 —5 —10		
OTHERS:							

NOTE: Incorrect engine —50, Rad. core (NA) —20, Starter added (NA) —10, Fuel supply device (NA) —10.

CLASS_____ MEET_____   DATE_____   PERFECT SCORE   **1000**

ENTRY NO._____ CAR_____   YEAR_____   ENTER total
points deducted

OWNER_____ ADDRESS_____

TEAM CAPT._____ DEPUTY JUDGE_____   GRAND SCORE

AWARD: JUNIOR; 1st, 2nd, 3rd, tied.

of all the hectic activity in the United States, takes place in Hershey, Pennsylvania, every October, near the national headquarters of the AACA. The car registration tally runs over 1,000; rare and wonderful Local, Regional, and National winners from all over the nation are driven and shipped in for this magnificent event. It can best be described as an admixture of mammoth art exhibit, royal coronation, and rip-roaring carnival, with a bit of gay masochism thrown in for good measure. The field glitters with great cars, the competition is unyielding, and the winners are ecstatic. This show represents the pinnacle of achievement for the best cars in the world.

So these are some of the challenges we faced for the future, as our knowledge of the hobby progressed. Going into our early shows, however, we knew little of the art beyond what our intelligence could supply.

Some hard decisions had to be made for the Alvis. Do we miss a couple of shows and dig in hard, or do we exhibit again soon and possibly suffer another irksome disappointment? We decided to wait and do further extensive work.

Chrome parts were removed all over the car; windshield frame, doorknobs, grille, hubcaps, bumpers. The Alvis then went to the upholsterer for new canvas top and carpeting. Agonizing problem: should we tear out the beautifully done gray British synthetic "leather" and replace with real leather? This we learned was worth five points (at about $500). We decided to wait on that! How about the paint? Could we repair cracks in the aluminum in small respray sections, or did we have to go all the way with a complete new lacquer paint job? Inquiries on this question shattered our enthusiasm. A top paint job then cost about $600. We quickly decided to patch and touch up.

Two months and $450 later, we registered for another Local but major show, this time in Miami, at Viscaya. Invariably, no matter how much advance time is devoted to show-prepping, somehow the night before the show is always spent on "final" details, after having *completed* "final details" all week long. (It's standard to get to bed about 2:00 A.M., exhausted, nerve-wracked, and despondent, swearing off it forever.)

A "must" rule is that *everything* is tested as another final check-out. Engine starting, lights, horn, windshield wipers, instruments—everything worked fine. The Alvis, however, always had a few tricks up her valve sleeves. On show morning, she wouldn't start! Now you may not believe this, but if you cuss loudly and angrily enough, you seem to ignite a spark, like flint against iron; she fires up, and you're finally on your way, with tools, lunch, and kids packed and rarin' to go. The Alvis was finally cowed into this state with indignation and a few violent kicks in the rear end.

Anyway, the second show ended the same as the first, with no award in our class. Our disillusionment was overpowering, though not yet lethal. But the Alvis was to suffer (psychologically).

We now viewed her distrustfully as an unyielding hostile element in our lives, and planned retribution, even though she *was* a marvelous car to drive. The only way to relegate her to minor position with us, we decided semi-humorously, was to buy *another* classic car! Since the fascination of the big European cars had taken hold of our fancies, we generally agreed to "specialize" in this difficult area of acquisition and restoration. Furthermore, having already become somewhat more sophisticated in the game, we also set another challenging limitation upon ourselves: to collect only "soft-top" models, such as roadsters, phaetons, tourers, and convertibles. A valid consideration in this choice (and let no collector state that he is not keenly aware of at least break-even resale value) is that open cars are usually worth about two to three times more than hardtop sedans and coupes. Rarely, however, does the private collector show a profit after the endless expenses of a *serious,* loving restoration.

The quest for "Number Two" began in the fall of 1964, via a steady flow of two-way correspondence flying across the Atlantic. One dealer in particular, with whom we were extremely impressed on our first visit, was Jack Bond, proprietor of Vintage Autos, Ltd. in Brooks Mews, London. Jack is a big, jolly, white-haired ex-actor Britisher who was among the earliest English dealers to recognize that Americans were easier to deal with and had a noticeable freedom of the checkbook. He offered the exotic type of machine that most interested us, generally a good cut above the average condition to be found at the time. His charming garage is in a tight cobblestone mews which is virtually landlocked at both ends, one end having a very narrow, downhill, stone tunnel leading in from the street, and the other, a tight, rakish, uphill "S" curve. We *never* dared to drive a big car out of either end, so he would always maneuver them out for test runs, and give me the wheel on the open streets outside the mews.

Jack's published motto is, "We don't deal in Bangers," a droll, typically British expression. He usually has four or five superb cars on display; we had several fine choices. A 1936, 4.5 liter Lagonda open-tourer with special "semi-boattail" caught our eyes the moment we entered the garage.

"Lagonda?" we asked uncertainly. "Is that an Italian car?"

Jack laughed, "That's a standard question. The designer of the Lagonda was an American who came over to England to work with the great racing car designers of the thirties. The name of his hometown was Lagonda, Ohio!"

This was almost too absurd to contemplate.

We then noticed a huge "Speed-Six" (6 1/2 liter) 1926 Bentley. This was one of the elite racing-touring automobiles of its day, spawned out of the mechanical genius of W. O. Bentley, who was then considered one of the three foremost engine designers in the world. "W. O.," as he was known to car buffs, had, since 1921, achieved worldwide recognition for his superb machines on the major European racing track circuit. (He died quietly in August of 1971, in a British nursing home at the age of 85.)

Eventually this emphasis on racing led "W. O." downhill to financial illiquidity despite the numerous superb touring automobiles he produced until 1931, at which time the Rolls Royce Company purchased all the Bentley assets and facilities, ending the era of a grand independent racing marque. Its absorption into Rolls changed its character almost completely. "W. O." then became a consultant to the Lagonda Company, working with Fred Meadows, and created the "Sanction" I, II, and III, which were all superlative automobiles between 1935 and 1939. The war ended this courtly series, and Lagonda was later acquired by Aston-Martin, with sporadic production after the war.

The 1926 six-liter Bentley monster lacked authenticity, as immediately discovered by Bobbie; in the development of an extensive home library, she had become an "aficionado" in the European marques. I depended upon her quick and alert instinct constantly, and still do. (Don't knock feminine intuition!)

Politely, but with a tone of authority, she pointed out, "This blower (supercharger) on the car must have been added later. Wasn't the first blown Bentley built in 1929?"

"That's almost right," Jack replied honestly. "The first blower appeared on experimental racing Bentleys in 1928."

This cooled us off somewhat, "authenticity" being a major judging point group. But at $4,500 the car was a steal anyway. Jack rolled the juggernaut out into the constricted mews, requiring three forward and three back-up maneuvers to head it out to the street. What a ride, the power and surge were unbelievable. Though the car was enormous in sheer bulk, the handling was silken. Bentley!

Jack came up with an enticing idea. "If you buy the Bentley *and* the Lagonda," he offered, "I'll have them both completely reupholstered with new Connolly 'Vaumol' leather, *and* new carpeting, at no extra charge."

"He's crazy" I thought wryly, "like a fox."

This reminded me of a favorite story from my Madison Avenue days. Two friends in the advertising game, meeting happily on the Avenue after many years of not encountering each other, started describing their intervening histories. After excitedly discussing their careers and families, one of them shyly stated that he now was raising baby elephants as a sideline. "How would *you* like to have a baby elephant?" he asked his old friend. The other, astonished, said, "Good Heavens, we're loaded now! We have four kids, two St. Bernards, a turtle, a cat, and three rabbits. What would I want with a baby elephant?"

His friend looked at him for a long searching moment. "Notwithstanding, I think you should hear me out. For you, old buddy as a *special* favor, how would you go for *two* elephants for the price of one?" he coaxed.

A long, painful silence followed; the air crackled. Out burst the incredible reply, "Now you're really talking! "

That's about how we reacted to the offer. Jack cleverly excused himself momentarily, and we looked at each other in a sidelong way. Bobbie, who is really the nuttier of the two of us, asked in a small, pipey voice, "With the new house ready in a few months, we'd have extra space for the pair, wouldn't we?"

I countered, "This giant would fill the garage like wall-to-wall carpeting! " But I knew our resistance was shot. A few minutes later, Jack wandered in from his office in the rear, and we tentatively accepted the irresistible offer, with the condition that we could have the option to change our minds about the Bentley before we left London, in about ten days.

At the time, I was quite busy in London at a U.S. trade show, exhibiting my company's products to European buyers. This didn't allow much time for car-hunting. However, the exhibit didn't open daily until 12:00 noon; that gave us some mornings free for comparison shopping. But unfortunately, there were no comparisons. A "Speed-Six" was a rare beast. We contacted the Rolls Royce Agency on Conduit Street. No, there was nothing like it available, to their best knowledge. But, they advised quickly, one of their

The 1924 3 liter Red Label Bentley, parked in the driveway of the previous owner in England.

salesmen owned a 1924 Red Label Bentley Van Den Plas 3-liter tourer, in beautifully restored condition. We left word for him to phone us at our hotel.

He turned out to be a young, pink-cheeked Englishman with impeccable manners. He confirmed, "I have a fine example of a 1924 'Red Label' Bentley, but at the moment I am holding a $500 deposit from Tony Curtis, your American movie star. He *was* due back from Rome three weeks ago to pick up the car and I'm certain to hear from him any day now." I caught the uncertainty in his voice, and with tigerish sales instinct, asked if we could possibly see the car anyway, just for the pleasure of it. He agreed to do this with typical British pride and courtesy.

The following morning he drove us out to his home in the suburbs. When he uncovered the lovely Bentley, we gasped. It was beautifully lacquered in black, with maroon wire wheels, and a long lean polished aluminum bonnet (hood). It was in marvelous condition, having recently had a complete engine rebuild, and was newly reupholstered, in red *vinyl!* "Here we go again," I thought resignedly, "it will need a complete leather renovation, or take a five-point loss in judging for the vinyl."

Despite this annoying problem, I put up a trial balloon to negotiate for the car, but Peter was a man of honor. He didn't see how he could sell us the

View of the gleaming aluminum bonnet of the Bentley, showing the big P-100 headlights.

car while holding a deposit from another collector, but he said if he hadn't heard from Curtis in the next eight days before we left for the Continent, he might then consider it differently. (He also revealed that he was being married in two weeks, and needed the cash badly.) So now, in a quandary, we possibly had *two* Bentleys on the hook. The 3-liter was a bit smaller, but notably more graceful than the "Speed-Six." It seemed to suit us better somehow.

The week rolled by with no word from Peter. We visited Jack Bond again and arranged for new red leather to be installed in the Lagonda (at extra cost, if we didn't also buy the "Six"). We forthrightly told him about the 3-liter, and the possibility of our buying it at a little less cost than the bigger car.

On Friday morning, the day before we were to leave London, Peter phoned us. He hadn't heard from Curtis, and had decided to sell us the car! We canceled our option with Jack Bond on the spot. (Four years later the "Speed-Six" was worth $20,000, our Red Label about *one-third* of that!)

POSTSCRIPTS BY MY WIFE

I remember the sure-thing preparations for our first few shows were so easy. *Sweet Innocence.*

The Alvis was "Alan's Car," and he did the polishing and heavy cleaning and all that sort of thing. I merely vacuumed the rugs and shined up the interior and dashboard. But by the second *show they had my dander up (not that it did any good). "What do they mean passing over our beautiful Alvis!" I thought indignantly. So I really began to look for trouble, and for what really was a prize-winning car, and how did we go about doing it, etc.*

From then on, I too was fully committed. I began to check colors of wires, I counted missing screws, I hunted for "wrong" hose-clamps, and painted all those silly thingamagigs that blow air into gas—carburetors? Never have been able to remember the names of the parts of an engine, but I sure know how to clean or polish or paint them. So I said determinedly to myself, authenticity is a big point winner, and I began an intensive program of research and reading that was to go on through the years. It made a studious librarian out of me; some big leap forward, from ballerina and professional dancing teacher to mechanical encyclopedia!

I remember, too, on that trip to England where we multiplied our troubles threefold by buying two more cars, something Peter said to us about the Bentley, which was like a personal forecast of the madness of the hobby. He said he never took his car out in the rain, but if he was ever caught in a drizzle he would duck under a railroad trestle or bridge or under some other cover and wait until the rain stopped, even if it took all *day. I thought then that this was a bit of charming British idiosyncrasy, but we found out later that it was a very good idea!*

About the Lagonda and the Bentley, I'll have more to say on those two dandies later, but I must admit I was as thrilled as a little girl who had just received her first toy stove. Just think of all the cakes and pies I could bake now!

3

Adventures as Importers

 I'll try to describe (without heaving emotion) the problems we had getting the Lagonda and the 3-liter Bentley delivered to the United States. A few high points in this delirium are worth telling.

When Jack Bond delivered the Lagonda to the upholsterer (trimmer, in England), unknown to him, this gentleman was on the verge of a nervous breakdown. For several weeks, the car disappeared and was finally found in a back alley by the police. Jack forced the issue, and after two months of unbelievable difficulties, he finally wrested it from the trimmer, not quite finished, and put it aboard a ship to Miami. During this time, three overseas phone calls were made (at about $20 each) plus a goodly number of cables.
I wrote to Jack:

> Your last letter tells an absolutely fantastic story about problems with Chris "B," the upholsterer.
>
> I can never adequately express my gratitude to you for the tremendous effort you put forth in finally getting my Lagonda on board the boat. You are certainly a superb businessman, and if ever you should need me to verify your integrity and reputation, you have only to ask for it and I will write a letter of recommendation par excellence.
>
> Naturally I was most grieved for you that you had such miseries with this man, "B." Let's hope that all of it will be worthwhile in allowing me to win in the coming concourse in Florida. . . .
>
> Again, let me say, you are a prince of a fellow!

To our surprise, when the car eventually did arrive, we were delighted with the pliant leather and craftsmanship, far superior to most upholstery work available in the States. We felt compensated for the headaches and anxieties.

The Bentley was still another story. (Dealing with an individual is quite different from buying from a recognized dealer like Bond, where you pay in toto for the car when purchased, without qualms.) A deposit had been left with Peter in June before we left London, and arrangements were made for final payment between Barclay's Bank and our bank, upon certified delivery documents in Miami.

During that summer of 1965 as we traveled around the Continent, we uneasily began to wonder if we should really have bought *two* cars (baby elephants). These misgivings mounted as the weeks passed, and by the time we returned to Miami we soberly felt that we could do without the Bentley. We wrote to Peter, and shamefacedly asked him to keep our $500 deposit. A wrathful reply arrived by Air Mail Special Delivery, warning us that if we reneged on the deal, he would go to the American Embassy and raise hell, etc. So—we apparently were to own the 3-liter Bentley! We were also somewhat wiser about British traditions, reactions, and sporting gestures. "After all, he did have to get married," we rationalized to each other.

The car arrived about a month later right in the middle of an East Coast dock strike. I stood languidly on the dock in Miami, trying to "see through" the steel hull for *just* a glimpse of the Bentley. Calls and conferences with dock officials were to no avail. Until the strike was settled, we were told snappily, there was no way on earth to release the car. Three weeks went by with no strike settlement in sight. Then, one day we received a phone call advising that the ship was departing for Mobile, Alabama, for unloading, about 700 miles from Miami.

We felt like the gluttons in the "Seven Deadly Sins" who were punished for their avarice by dying of indigestion. Off I went to Alabama by plane. Arguments, endless entreaties; the car was documented to be delivered to Miami, the dock people said stubbornly, and we would have to wait for the ship to return to Miami at some undetermined date. Several $20 bills changed hands lightning-fast. Soon, the Bentley (which had luckily been stored in the hold in an open channel) was slung out in a huge crane and settled with a bump on the dock. I had gruesome memories of the Alvis airplane delivery.

Arrangements were made with a commercial truck line ($310) for the

Bentley to be delivered to the rear dock of my factory in Hialeah, Florida. Thus, without further woes the unique delivery saga of the Bentley ended.

But that was only the beginning of our encroaching problem.

We now had three cars, relatively unprotected, under the carport in our old house. What to do? A good friend and fellow club member who lived in a charming converted farmhouse with ample barn space agreed to store the Bentley. It remained in his barn for more than six months, while we settled into the new house and got fully organized. Then we brought it home and put it in the garage.

Our first choice on the action front: restoration on the Lagonda. Chrome "disassembly" was initiated; engine "cosmetics" were undertaken. Points for engine compartment authenticity and appearance are as critical as any other area of a show car. Over the years the succession of owners understandably bastardize and modernize engines for their convenience, with never a thought about the future, or about the correctness or appearance of wiring, carburetors, magnetos, and the like. After all, the British contend, why bother, for daily use?

Conversely, to prepare for show, an antique or classic automobile *must* be brought back as near as possible to its original state. This means an endless hunt for authentic parts, colors, materials, and painstaking detailing. It's tough enough to do this with American cars, twice as difficult with European cars. Thankfully, Bobbie is mostly in charge of these activities; how many times has she been found hanging over a side-mount wheel, her head deep in the engine, legs askew, working with sable paint brushes and writing checklists for parts to be found.

While all these pursuits were going on, car shows came up regularly in Miami, Fort Lauderdale, and Palm Beach. We attended all with zeal, showing either the Alvis or the Lagonda. The Alvis had not yet won a trophy in three shows, so we reluctantly decided at last to do a complete body-and-paint restoration, and to display the Lagonda with whatever partial work we had already completed. (This abdication was to pay off with more than a year of show disappointments with the Lagonda—though we did take one third prize—swimming salmon-style against the awards current until we could give her our undivided attention.) On top of that the Bentley was soon to start clamoring for a thorough "fine point" going-over. But *first,* the Alvis! we said. We sure had our hands full in 1965-1966.

Finding a good car painter in Miami is as likely as discovering an original Rembrandt in a hut on Guadalcanal. There are only a handful of paint and body shops that do meticulous work, but most of them don't want to *touch* a "classic" job. Eventually, we found a shop in Hialeah reputed to do good custom work, and after intensive discussions and price-haggling, we delivered the Alvis with a prayer. This was our first of many hair-whitening experiences with car painters.

The big spring show of 1966 at Viscaya was about four weeks away, and, foolishly, we felt rather secure with the schedule. It was too late to test the water with our toes; we now had to take the plunge on a major body restoration.

In retrospect, we admit to being incredibly naive about this major service. Later experience was to prove that 4 *months* was more accurate a time schedule than 4 *weeks*. But we airily took it for granted, much as you would when buying a set of new tires; you pay the bill and depart when they're mounted.

The initial warning of trouble flared up on my first visit to the paint shop, about two weeks later. Although the body had been filled and sanded, and partially primed, the workmanship was woefully inadequate. I was shocked, and said so *very* carefully. Even my controlled remark infuriated the owner. His attack was totally unexpected, fierce, and exaggerated.

"Take your goddam car outa' here," he yelled. "You crazy car collectors expect us to stop our other work and put all our time into your damn heaps!"

I was staggered, and for the moment quite tongue-tied. I also fortunately stopped to think of the consequences, and kept my tongue tied.

The unreasonableness of this charge stemmed, I guessed, from his growing realization that the aluminum body had given up its infinite secrets of age only *after* the paint was removed. Instead of what he must have planned, i.e., to do a basic sanding and resurfacing, numerous cracks and ripples had unexpectedly leaked through. I quietly reminded him that he was the expert, and that we had a written contract to complete the car in time for the show.

Still angry, he replied, "You're gonna' have to pay a lot more than we estimated, or take me to court!"

I knew I was whipped; he had me on a tight schedule, and there was no other place to go. "How much more?" I asked resignedly.

"About two hundred bucks more, that's how much," he snarled, obviously daring me to drive the car away unfinished.

We settled finally on a split of $100 additional. He warned me emphatically not to bother him again until a few days before the show. It was now

The "Iron Duke" with costumed crew at the Vizcaya show

1934 Aston-Martin Mark II Short Chassis Racer

quite clear that we faced another probable failure with the Alvis, and at best, the job could not possibly be up to the high standards we had envisioned.

My next visit fully confirmed these fears; although the car was almost completed, the paint was dull and grainy, and hairline cracks still showed at certain angles of light. The refinished chrome parts I had delivered were still in boxes; no attempt had been made to reinstall even the smallest items.

What we did then is what we had to do on three other paint restorations in the future: we gathered a crew of friends to help us finish the job! We couldn't possibly have made the deadline otherwise. Two solid nights of tedious labor, paint rubbing, and parts replacement brought us up to 2:00 A.M. of the show morning. Exhausted and disgusted, we walked into the owner's office where he lay asleep on a battered old couch. I pulled out my checkbook and asked for the bill.

"I won't take your check!" was his amazing statement.

Stuttering with indignation, I asked where he expected me to get $500 in currency at 2:00 A.M. on a Saturday morning.

"That's your problem!" he shouted. "This car is not movin' outa' here until I get my cash!"

The situation was admittedly revolting, and Bobbie began to cry with frustration. Arguments, assurances, explanations were useless. (Looking back at this incredible experience, many years later, we still can't find any forgiveness or humor in the episode.) Angrily, I reached for the phone and started dialing the police. He grabbed it from my hand, and slammed it down violently.

We stalked out of the garage, praying fervently that he wouldn't lock the doors behind us, and started hunting for a phone booth. We finally phoned the police from a nearby all-night gas station. Within a few minutes a patrol car arrived. After hearing our story, the police sadly advised that the problem was entirely out of their jurisdiction. We asked if they would at least help us to reason with the man since it was now close to 3:00 A.M. This they agreed to do, and after lengthy discussion, while we stood aside, the owner relented slightly. "I'll take your check if you leave enough security," he said arrogantly. "Then you can bring me the cash on Monday, and I'll return the security."

We started to ransom the Alvis. Together we had about $250 in cash. That plus a check, plus my Omega watch, a ring, and other incidental jewelry completed the incongruous transaction. The deal was written up on a billhead, witnessed by the police, and we at last nervously drove the Alvis home in the near-dawn of the balmy spring morning.

After three hours of restless sleep we staggered out of bed, still aching and tasting unseasoned mayhem. We had planned to take three cars for judging to this nearby show at Viscaya; both the Bentley and the Lagonda had been prepared to our maximum ability in the time available while the Alvis was in the paint shop. Bobbie and I each drove a car, and the third was ferried by a friend.

Viscaya is one of Miami's major permanent tourist attractions. It was bequeathed to the city by members of the Deering family. A magnificent reproduction of a huge Italian villa, it was constructed in 1914-1916 on a long, beautifully situated strip of verdant land directly on Biscayne Bay. The furnishings and sculptures were selected by experts in Italy. With its carefully tended formal gardens and exquisite lawns, Viscaya makes a unique and gorgeous setting for an antique car show.

Arriving with three cars in our own private parade, we were directed to a stepped-up plateau of grass, surrounded by statuary and fountains, where we had an exclusive show area all to ourselves. The freshly painted Alvis, now black and cream, with new wide-whitewall tires, new black canvas top, and sharp rechroming, looked pretty good from a short distance away (if one didn't get too close to the paint job). The other two cars glittered in the May sunlight, and were it not for our bizarre memories of the night before, we might well have been able to enjoy the colorful activities.

One of the amusing special events at the meet was a costume-judging contest. Despite the trying emotional strain of the prior week, Bobbie had gamely conjured up a sweeping black gown of the thirties, with a huge velvet picture hat we had found in Spain the summer before. It was even big enough to cover her pallor! For my part, a huge paste-on walrus mustache covered the twitch of anger in my upper lip, and my Chaplinesque costume consisted of an old pair of wide-bottom trousers, short black alpaca coat, a gray silk ascot, and a derby hat.

The absurdity of my attire helped relieve our nervous tension, and we joined the groups of other club members in their attic-extracted lace and velvet gowns, flowered hats, and lace-up, high-button shoes. There were flapper-length satin dresses, egret feathered headbands, gleaming jeweled clasps, ropes of beads. The men variously wore green-checkered, tightly-fitted suits, cutaway coats, knickers, argyle stockings, and derbies. The gaiety, color, and excitement blended perfectly into the romantic atmosphere at Viscaya. Here, in an environment of yesteryear, on the elegant grounds surrounded by the polished old cars and grand costumes, you could easily feel transported into the past.

Later, I felt buried in the present, as our Herculean efforts with the Alvis grudgingly yielded a Third Place trophy, admittedly against very stiff competition in the classic category. The Bentley and the Lagonda, while greatly admired by the public, went unheralded by the judges. We hadn't *really* expected to place with these two yet unfinished beauties, but we'd show 'em!

POSTSCRIPTS BY MY WIFE

The adventures of getting our classic cars from Europe to where we live, right from the first one we bought, have all been Hairbreadth Harry. But admittedly the travels and travails of the Lagonda and the Bentley stand alone in their niches of infamy.

After the Iron Duke (my name for the Lagonda) was released from Bondage, he made it home safely and with dignity, like the aristocrat he was. But the Lady B. gave us a good run for our money. Do you know, that agonizing dock strike lifted for one day, and they started to unload the ship, but something else happened and the stevedores went on strike again just as they were getting to the cars in the hold. So off she went to Alabama. She must have been quite a flirt in her day; capriciously for no reason at all, she took off on a quick trip to Mobile.

Oh, but for pure undistilled pain and fury, the Alvis paint job wins hands down. All the final work we had planned to do at home had to be done at that dreadful, hostile man's garage. For instance—there were long aluminum channels on the running board with black rubber strips in them. These had been removed on the assumption that they would be replaced by the shop men. The metal strips had been straightened and buffed, and I had cleaned and freshened up the rubber, as new ones were not to be found anywhere. It was almost midnight of the last night before I could get busy to reinstall them. I sat on the cold concrete floor trying to match strips and holes and rubbers, and pushing the rubbers back into the channels until my fingers were sore and blistered.

We fought that job down to the wire, and if I'd been an hysterical type I'd have had a bawl that night!

4

The Taste of Blood

The next major meet on the schedule was the Classic Car Club of America Show in Cypress Gardens, Florida. We went to work on the Lagonda with fierce vigor, having by now accepted the fact that the Alvis had limped to its peak, at least with *us* as its owners. We recognized that a point of no return exists with any one car owned by a collector, where subtle discouragements and repeated disappointments add up to an overwhelming lassitude, and that's the time to sell the car.

The Alvis, splendid piece that she was, was sold to an oil man in Tulsa via an advertisement in the quarterly AACA magazine. Goodbye, First-born! The day she was driven away from our home (by the professional driver who had flown to Miami for the new owner) sticks in our memory with particular sentiment. We have bought, restored, and sold many other cars since then, but the graceful, sleek Alvis was our first (we took a loss), and therefore somehow special. As she disappeared over the curve at the top of our street, we all stood in the driveway, lumps in throat, waving goodbye. For a day or two all of us, including the boys, were a bit moony until we received a wire from the buyer that she had made the trip all the way to Oklahoma in twenty-eight hours without incident, thoroughbred that she was! Several months later we heard a rumor that she had taken a First Prize in a meet at Dallas, and assumed that the new owner had patiently brought her up to her rightful status. (The feeling of participation in an eventual win with "one of our cars" is still deeply satisfying.) This sharpened our resolve to make the Lagonda a top trophy-winner, and we set to this task with gusto. With the exception of a few tiny nicks and dings in the fender, the body and paint were in excellent condition. This was quite a simple matter to correct. With a few more chrome parts replated, and some engine cosmetics finished, we were ready for Cypress Gardens, and we hoped, the coveted Winner's Circle.

The grounds of this famous tourist spot are beautifully landscaped, surrounding a sparkling lake, with moss-hung cypress trees standing knee-deep in the water along the shore. But it was not until several years later that a fine hotel was built inside the compound, so the meet was held in the parking lot of the nearby village shopping center. It was midsummer, and unless you too have been parked for hours on blacktop, in the middle of August in Florida, the incredible buildup of heat is indescribable. At fair estimate, exposed to the blazing tropical sun, the "reflected temperature" reading can go as high as 120°! At least two hours were to elapse between lineup and judging time, so we made it tolerable with repeated visits to the drugstore soda fountain, sojourns to the air-conditioned shops, and lunch in the cool cafeteria. To our chagrin, returning from lunch we learned that the Lagonda judging had unexpectedly been done during our absence. Without the owner on hand, all 'mechanical and running' points had been passed over! We rushed out to find the judges, and cajoled them into returning to the car. Otherwise, all these vital points would have been lost forever, including starting, idle, brakes, lights, horn, wipers, and instruments. Luckily, all these functions were perfect, a very important factor in our final score.

Our competition that day was most respectable. Approximately ten other cars in this big car luxury category had us hopping all morning, doing our own pre-judging evaluations. We grimly acknowledged that there were some great high-point winners we had to beat, including the renowned 1929 Lincoln Landaulet that had taken every important trophy at Viscaya not long before. In all honesty, to compete with these champions made us wonder if we would even place within the top three positions. The unknown factor we were counting on was the mechanical group; in those shows that do judge these "working" items they can be the make-or-break in the score, since no owner can possibly predict the spiteful behavior of his car at the moment of truth.

That evening, showered, cooled, and dressed for the occasion, we sipped cocktails with a group of friends before the awards banquet. (Bobbie wore white gloves throughout the dinner to conceal her broken fingernails and grime-caked hands, not an uncommon sight among those good ladies who dig in with their husbands, degreasing and polishing before a show.) We tried to remain calm as the awards announcements started. Eventually—you can't

The 1936 4.5 liter Lagonda, the "Iron Duke," at Cypress Gardens before the start of the Meet.

rush it—our class was called. Third prize went to a '34 Rolls Royce. Second prize went to the famed Lincoln. We waited breathlessly, pulses racing. At that particular point, the awarding judge remembered an anecdote about an old Lincoln, and for the next five minutes—it seemed like five years—we remained numb and glassy-eyed waiting for the interminable tale to come to an end. Then came the sweetest music this side of heaven, since Guy Lombardo. "First Prize to Alan Radcliff's magnificent Lagonda!"

I remained glued to my seat. Here at last was the dreamed-of moment, and I was totally paralyzed. Bobbie pinched me. I bounded to my feet, trotted up to the podium, and almost by reflex turned to the crowd. "This award goes to my wife Barbara, in recognition of her unrestorable hands!" I called out happily.

Finally, after almost two years of ardent, bonded indenture and anticipation, we were in that Inner Circle of First Prize Winners. And too, we had beaten that unbeatable Lincoln.

There is a "feeling" among antique and classic car restorers that once you break the ice with a top trophy in a big show, you're in real trouble, as nothing else will satisfy you. This is a very dangerous frame of mind, since

Lagonda engine compartment, ready for judging, polished and gleaming.

there is always that newer car *someone else* is working on, while your prize winner is getting nicked, baked, and tired dragging around to the frequent shows. To stay on your guard is the rule—get cocky and you end up like the Lincoln; poor Doc Jacobsen, he sold her soon afterward.

POSTSCRIPTS BY MY WIFE

One of the first things I discovered about a show car is that the undersides were almost as important as the uppersides, pretty much like a new baby, messy diapers and all.

There must be no rust, no loose wiring or shabby dust pans, and a minimum of grease and grime, so you can get your fresh paint job on the chassis and the other gadgets underneath. Alan, all 6' 2" and 200 pounds of him, has a trick lower sacroiliac, and is therefore unable to stoop or bend for any length of time—at least that's what he's always told me. So even though the initial major steam-cleaning and descaling job is usually done at a commercial place, someone still has to keep checking underneath, and at the very least the muffler and pipes always need refreshing. That's for lucky me. And heaven forbid we should lose points in my *department!*

The drive with the Lagonda from Miami to Cypress Gardens was quite a long haul for the massive Iron Duke. His gray suit of armor matched his formidable appearance. No "she" was this robust chap, and luckily so. It was August and the Florida sun was really a ball of fire in the sky. We started out with the top up for shade, but sides wide open for the breeze. Most vintage English cars had no heaters, even in England they didn't need them! All the engine heat came blasting into the cockpit anyway. Just what we needed for the long summer trip!

About halfway there, the skies opened up with a rumble and a cooling, welcome downpour. Being an open-tourer, the Duke had nothing so mundane as windows, so everybody got out to try to jigsaw puzzle the side curtains into place, getting good and wet in the process. But side curtains will never replace windows. They leak and flap and flutter and there's no way to let in some air without letting in some rain, and pretty soon the car feels like a steambath. Then you try holding open the little hand signal flap opening, and you get a stream of water up your sleeve. It's no fun, let me tell you. But rain too shall pass, and it did cool off the road, the engine, and the canvas top. All I could think of miserably was, "Oh that undercarriage. It must be filthy!" I consoled myself with the further thought that it was only water and could be washed off. Thirty miles later I wasn't so happy. We hit a stretch of freshly tarred road, and I could hear it pinging and splattering up on my "freshly laundered underthings."

We got to Cypress Gardens about nightfall and checked into our motel. It was too late to do anymore than wash down the Duke, splash the hose around underneath, and hope for the best—or, I should say, the least. Seven o'clock the next morning I was spread out underneath the car cleaning off the tar with mineral spirits (we always carried a load of supplies) and trying to degrime the tire wells and under the fenders. Alan and our older boy, Jonathan, were up front cleaning the chrome, fighting to polish out the paste of road dirt and tar. We made it just in time for the lineup, but as usual there was no time for me to restore my hands! Did that really matter?

The morning was busy with parading, judging, checking out the competition, and cooling off in the shops. It's all very enjoyable, and everyone is gay (or pretending to be gay) while keeping an eye peeled for the judges. We usually leave one of us on guard at the car for Prevention. Innocent-looking sightseers love to fondle the fenders or doors and inevitably leave nicks and scratches from rings, belt buckles, or handbags. We have a collection of warning signs to stick on the windows, the one we like best is:

UNLESS You Are In The

NUDE!

Please DO NOT Lean On This Car!

Buttons and Belt Buckles SCRATCH!

Award banquet time came, so I pulled on my white gloves. Did you ever try to eat a buffet dinner with gloves on; did you ever take a bath with socks on? The standing joke was, "The car is gorgeous, but only 30 points for the hands." But none of that touched my spirit. We finally took our First Place for the Lagonda, and that's the real payoff.

I've often wondered if we had won just a little something the first time out with the Alvis, whether we would ever have felt so jubilant about winning thereafter.

5

The Bentley Catches It

 It was now time to apply our attentions to the Red Label Bentley tourer. Typically, having been restored in England, great devotion had been given to her engine. It gleamed in pristine beauty, chrome-polished engine plates, et al. Mechanically she was almost perfect, although on hearing that she was equipped with a racing-type "crash" gearbox you might wonder if all was well. This simply means that on every gear change a grinding, gnashing roar occurs, absolutely normal, but quite nerve-shattering. We never became fully accustomed to this arm-jarring jackhammer, but after changing to different gear oil twice, we discovered that this idiosyncrasy was quite standard, and crashed our way through the changes, wincing every time!

The first task in seeking point improvement was obviously the replacement of the red vinyl upholstery and the rather coarse, black carpets. It's always difficult to understand why the English would use vinyl with all that delectable leather available in England while only effecting a very small economy. (All the labor involved in a total upholstery job goes down the drain when the vinyl is ripped out mercilessly, and this is exactly what we had to do.) Working very closely with our custom upholsterer in South Miami, we selected a tough-grained black cowhide, and began research on the precise spacing of the pleats, type of front bucket seats, door panel treatment, and other related details. Fortunately we were able to find photographs in our home library which clearly showed the interior arrangement and seat contours. We discovered to our distress that our Bentley's front bucket seats were the wrong shape and size; after tearing off the covering and padding, we came up with strange-looking aluminum frames that ob-

Bentley engine compartment, showing copper-plated vacuum tank upper left, and polished S.U. carburetor bowls.

viously needed major reshaping. This turned out to be a rough task, but after much filing and metal cutting, the skeleton shape began to resemble the photos.

The Bentley then remained in the leather shop for almost three months undergoing the interior renovation. Near the end of the conversion job, we suddenly thought about installing the canvas hood. Naturally, and consistent with other adventures in English car restoration, the damned thing didn't fit. Although the black canvas was quite new and of good quality, seemingly perfect in its neatly folded condition, it simply did not fit the braces or fastenings that came with the car! This painful development forced us into further research. More photos were examined under a magnifying glass, sketches were drawn and redrawn. The necessary decision had to be made to rebuild the entire strut-support system, along with having all new canvas fitted to the car. In addition, a new front wood bow was also needed to fit over the windshield posts. This was created from a fine thick plank of oak, carefully shaped to the window frame, as always at considerable expense. The tubular steel center and rear braces were recut to fit the body contours, and all fasteners remachined to finish the job. Several weeks later, we congratulated ourselves on a marvelous achievement. Our dingy old photos, plus a well of determination, had broken a major impasse.

The next area to be tackled was the instrument panel. This needed only refinishing of the mahogany surface and installation of a new speedometer cable. Then with some minor touch-up of the exterior paint surfaces and a bit of chrome work, we felt ready for competition.

In keeping with our other foolhardy enthusiasms, we had become intrigued with the idea of obtaining a trailer to enable us to attend the longer-distance shows upstate and in neighboring states. We had reached a point in ardor and competitiveness that compelled us to range far and wide in the showing of the Lagonda and the Bentley. The search for a special trailer to carry these large cars drove us disappointingly into one dead end after another. The logical solution therefore (what else!) was to have one custom-built. As Mr. Blanding learned thoroughly when rebuilding his Dream House, courage, perseverence, blind confidence, and idiocy are the minimum prerequisites. We therefore plunged energetically into the design and construction of this vehicle, working closely with a reputable custom builder of rolling stock. Not being half-measure minded, we decided to color-coordinate this carrier to the Bentley, with red wheels, black lacquered fenders, and silver trim.

The problems that developed on this project further strained our sanity. We were in constant conference about mathematical weight balances, angle of ramps, tie-down systems, length of tow bar, overall dimensions. Without technical background to draw upon, we had to accede to the opinions of the builder about electric brakes and stop lights, wind-up winches, and steel structural members. Weeks became months during this phase of our education. Finally "Hairbreadth Harvey," our massive trailer, stood completed, just in the nick of time for the annual Birthplace of Speed meet in Ormond Beach, Florida, a historic gathering place on the sands of the famous Daytona auto racing beaches.

Feeling absolutely secure in the knowledge that we had "spared no horses" in the design and construction essentials, including mobile-home heavy duty wheels, tires, and brakes, and jack up front end tow bar, we joyfully loaded and secured the Bentley, hooked it up to our station wagon's specially built towing hitch, and started off on the 350 mile trip. The first few cautious miles in local traffic gave us a misleading sense of euphoria. The hand brake control worked smoothly, the whole rig felt like a heavy-gauge

The Bentley on its color-matched, custom-built trailer just before its first trip to the Ormond Beach "Birthplace of Speed" Meet.

diesel railroad train. We wheeled up onto the Sunshine Parkway pushing like old pros. The clanking and mild bounding was disconcerting for awhile at higher speeds, but we had been told that was normally to be expected. During the first thirty miles I held the speed to about 50 miles per hour. As my confidence grew I concluded that 60 was the safe maximum range, which was based on advice from the designer. So I let go.

We were caught suddenly in a gusty side wind, and the trailer started to sway slightly. Alarmed and forgetful, instead of remembering the cardinal rule to use the trailer brakes, *not the car brakes,* I applied slight pressure to the foot brake. All hell broke loose at once. In a few paralyzing seconds that followed, the swaying increased violently, the landscape became a blur, and then, with a mad lunge and a leap, the huge trailer jackknifed behind us, swinging almost completely around. We landed with a jolt on the center median, the car facing south, the trailer facing north, but still hooked up to each other. Petrified and dazed, as through a blurry glass, I watched a hubcap careen crazily across the southbound lane. Bobbie had a weird reaction to this. "There goes our hubcap," she yelled. Before I could move to prevent it, she bolted out of the car and raced across the moving traffic lane as though the only thing in life that mattered at that moment was retrieving that ridiculous, wobbling hubcap. She breathlessly jumped back into the car a moment later, clutching her prize.

It seemed an eternity before I fully realized what had happened. The boys in the back seat were trembling, silent and stiff with fear. My moist hands were still locked on the steering wheel. I reacted.

"We're going home!" I yelled. "When we get home this damned trailer is going on the auction block!"

Still in shock, but holding her prized hubcap, Bobbie wailed. "How can we quit now after all the grief of getting ready for this show?"

I glared at her in astonishment. What a display of guts! "Are you nuts? We could all get killed with this monster behind us!"

She tried her most reasonable, coaxing tone. "Maybe we have the Bentley loaded off the center of gravity," she said with a catch in her voice. "Let's pull off the parkway and see what's wrong."

We sat there for awhile, not speaking, thinking and gathering our wits. I started the motor; it purred as though nothing at all had happened. Nervously, I eased the rig into a gap in traffic, the trailer following meekly out of its jackknifed position, heading south and homeward.

Never tempt the gods, I thought grimly. "We're going home," I said again, with jaw set.

But Bobbie wouldn't give up. She argued that we owed it to ourselves to check out the loading position of the Bentley, that maybe by making some simple adjustments, we would solve the problem, etc., etc. Having calmed down a bit, I found again that at lower speeds the rig could be controlled nicely with cautious use of the electric hand brake. Grudgingly, though against my better judgment, I wondered if she was right after all. About five miles south of the appalling incident, with ambivalent emotions, I pulled off the expressway and rolled into a gas station.

The instant we explained what had happened, experts sprang up all around us. Together, we moved the car slightly forward on the trailer and tied down the Bentley so the load was over the tandem wheels "where it was supposed to be," according to some helpful, straw-chewing, armchair generals. Ten minutes later, filled with misgivings, I entered the fast moving traffic lane *headed north* again, and discovered that a freshened breeze had started blowing during our session with the weight balancing. Despite the repositioning of the Bentley, some sway was soon apparent, though controllable. I slowed down regularly with the electric braking system, averaging about 45 miles an hour. At that rate, since it was already noontime and we were still about 300 miles from our destination, we theorized that we would surely miss the Friday evening cocktail party and pre-show festivities. (Both boys had caucused earlier with their mother and voted with her to go on, and they now agreed that it was better to be slow and steady than quit. The real objective of competing in the meet itself on Saturday morning was obviously what mattered.)

Unhappily, as we drove farther on the expressway into the open unprotected countryside, the breeze increased to a moderately gusty wind force. With our double length broadside to the wind, the swaying increased noticeably, and though I no longer had the fear of losing control, it was very tense driving.

Suddenly a State Trooper drew up alongside and flagged us off the road. "What now?" I groaned.

"What's wrong with your trailer?" he demanded. "Your swaying is dangerous to other traffic!"

I explained that I was on my way to a car show, proceeding cautiously. He walked around the rig and came back to the car window.

"Your antique car is loaded poorly," he said with definite authority. "The wind force is stronger than the momentum of your forward motion. You'll have to get off the parkway and continue on U.S. 1 where you'll have some protection from the buildings and the lower speed limits." Then he added as an afterthought, "Don't try getting back on the parkway later. I'm going to call ahead and alert the other patrol cars."

I ached at the thought of threading our way laboriously all the way up and beyond Daytona Beach, but the conservative side of my nature sighed with relief. With no further trouble, but totally exhausted, we pulled into our hotel at 9:00 P.M., bleary-eyed and stiff, but really pleased that we had turned back north. Without my wife's strength of purpose (and obvious confidence in me) we would *certainly* have quit and gone home.

Results: despite all the work on the Bentley, the dreadful experience on the road, and all our high hopes, we only placed Third in our class, and received a green satin *ribbon* for our trouble. At least it could have been *blue*!

POSTSCRIPTS BY MY WIFE

While the poor Bentley sat half-dressed at the upholstery shop, I decided to take advantage of the situation to paint some interior metal and wood surfaces under the instrument panel. No one ever sees it, but one of the objects of the sport is to preserve these great automobiles. The best way to make sure nothing will rust or rot is from within.

George, our favorite upholsterer, is a fine gentleman and runs a nice clean shop. Armed with paints and brushes, wearing a pair of Jon's dungarees, one of his old shirts, and dirty old tennis sneakers, I was having a good time for myself. Most restoration jobs are not really too hard, but getting under the dashboard takes a little special female maneuvering. Upside down with your shoulders on the floor, your derrière on the seat, and your legs extending out over the door in a Late Gothic "S" Curve, you can reach almost everywhere under the dash. Of course you get some paint on your nose and in your hair, but if you can stand the crazy position for half an hour, you've got it made.

While I was busily engrossed in my work, I heard voices in the shop near the Bentley, where before there had been only soft music from the radio and the industrious tapping of hammers or the whir of the sewing machine. I could hear some man getting an estimate from George, describing how his convertible top had been destroyed by vandals. The story was long, loud, and laced with strong language and a few choice four-letter words. I had just finished my tasks, uncurled myself from beneath the dashboard and rolled out of the car. The man's eyes grew round, he went pink, and his mouth fell open. "Migod," he stammered, "that was a woman under there!"

I don't know if George got the job—he was pretty shook up himself—for the man stumbled out of there red-faced and abashed. I guess he didn't believe in equal job opportunities for women.

My terrible memories of our trip to Ormond Beach are still like a nightmare. When the trailer jackknifed, I remember throwing myself toward the center of the car as my door flew open. I remember yelling to the boys in the back seat to hang on. After my stupid compulsive recovery of the rolling hubcap, I stood beside the car quivering and saw an absolutely waxen husband still clutching the wheel, and two small boys, who for once had nothing to say. My first two thoughts were a prayer of thanksgiving (it was Thanksgiving weekend), and then, "How did it happen?" I don't remember where I got the courage to want to go on, but I just knew we couldn't let all our work go to waste.

We had another misery that Alan obviously wants to repress. The next day after we had our turkey dinner, Alan began to have nausea and stomach cramps, probably in part a reaction to the trailer debacle, or to a virus. None of us others were affected, but he felt absolutely miserable. This meant he couldn't take the Bentley down to the hard-packed beach for the afternoon antique car races, and this was another big disappointment to him. I certainly couldn't do it, because her crash gear box drove my leg back from the clutch into my stomach every time I shifted gears. Without racing, we automatically lost out at a chance for the coveted Miller Trophy, a special award given at this show to the best all-round antique racing-type automobile.

It was also just our luck that one of our judges in the "racer" class was a perfectionist, and though he restored cars of his own, he loved to pick others apart; only his *cars were perfect. He made a big deal over some exposed nailheads in the new side panel leather.*

Right up to the moment of departure on Sunday morning, after the awards ceremony, Alan was still upchucking behind the trees, and I had to get some of our Miami car friends to help load the Bentley on the trailer. It was a pretty subdued family that drove home on that long day. We've never taken another car to "The Birthplace of Speed" show again. I wonder why?

6

Growing Up

 After the near-calamity and tortured northward trip with the trailer, and a sort of tiptoeing 8-hour trip coming home Sunday, we thoughtfully reevaluated our attitude about "trailering" long distance. We agreed, after some painful discussion, that the long hauls should not be undertaken again. (We did use the trailer again, *once*, for a short run to a meet in Palm Beach; more about that later.) We also found out, to our mixed chagrin and relief, that the Lagonda would not fit comfortably on the trailer tracks. It was wider than the Bentley, and the one attempt we made to load the Duke on the carrier clearly indicated that we would mash the fenders getting aboard.

Our next show with the Lagonda was in Fort Lauderdale. It was a hot steamy South Florida day in early fall, and it poured solid sheets of rain on the way up. As noted before, side curtains on vintage cars are mostly a farce for protection (how did people ever live with them?), and we ended up stuffing rags and Kleenex tissues under the windshield and around the plastic snap-on curtains. We still got trickles inside, and the car was a mess inside and out by the time we arrived at the show grounds. When you think of the hours spent cleaning the undercarriage before a meet, how can you bear the mud and road grime dripping from the frame? We left early, not expecting to win at all, and we were surprised and pleased to receive a phone call on Sunday telling us that we had won Second Place. Other cars arriving earlier, or having been under cover all night, had their opportunity to clean up underneath. We properly assumed that this was to their advantage.

Our collection of trophies and show plaques at this point in 1967 was becoming quite respectable, and we had gained a nice reputation for our "unusual" cars. Our special category of the luxury cars, which certainly enhances any show, also carried its own peculiar inherent problems. While they won't ever admit it openly, I feel that collectors of Fords and other relatively "simple" American vintages covertly feel animosity toward owners of the "big" cars, particularly the glamorous European marques. This evidences itself in vague subconscious promptings. Trying to judge a Lagonda by *Ford* standards is obviously absurd, but unfortunately there are not enough experienced judges who really understand the great foreign classics. During judging the owner stands aside, prepared to answer questions. It's quite an ordeal to restrain yourself when the nit-picking begins. At one big show, for instance, a consistent prize-winning, Ford-owner judge got down under the Lagonda, glanced around at the undercarriage, triumphantly raised his head, and bellowed, "Ha Ha! Two screws missing on the splash pan!" I would have slunk away in the tall grass if there had been any nearby. The shameful feeling of guilt is ridiculous, not to mention the sinking feeling about the point loss.

Car judging, in my humble opinion, should be a matter of simple humanity! We need an ASPCC (American Society for Prevention of Cruelty to Collectors). In my own judging experience over the years, I have always tilted backwards to be kind to the owner, emphatically recognizing the enormous devotion and reverence given to restoration. In some instances I must admit I may have even transgressed the holy boundaries of Judgmanship by offering unsolicited sotto voce suggestions for future improvements. (This is considered verboten, but what the heck, it's only a hobby!)

I recall the incident vividly that really put me on the griddle. Two beautiful, almost 100-point-perfect cars, a magnificent 1929 Packard short-chassis roadster, and an elegant 1929 Lincoln Sedanca Limousine, were vying in the same class for First Prize. The judging panel was composed of five men, with myself at the head. We had completed judging the class and faced the dilemma of the First and Second Place decisions. Both great cars were found to have achieved 99 1/2 points, itself a minor miracle. The Packard, newly finished for this show, had lost its half point for a pinpoint burr on a chrome windshield post. The Lincoln fell short of a 100 for a "browny" spot on the *inside* end curve of its rear bumper. In a clinch, at a time like this, other factors need to be considered. The Lincoln had recently been professionally restored at great expense by a commercial restorer, while the Packard had been wonderously remade by its amateur owner. To me this was to be a fine deciding factor, but since no rule exists about "amateur" versus "professional" restoration, the decision could not openly be made on this basis. Psychologically, judges being human (sometimes), this important fact may creep into the verdict.

A tight tie score like this requires a second thorough reexamination of both cars. After intensive searching, I found a tiny rough spot in the middle of the Lincoln's coated-fabric "leatherette" roof covering—this was a sure 1/2 point loss. I showed it to the other four judges; they agreed. The Packard emerged the winner. I believe to this day that the owner of the Lincoln never forgave me for this bit of super-sleuthing, and in a later show where he was judging one of *my* cars, he reciprocated the favor on a tight decision; my car took Second Place by one point! Can I say for certain that this clubby vendetta was a figment of my imagination?

We went off to Europe again in the summer of 1967. One of England's finest dealers, Dale's Stepsons in London, is renowned for Rolls Royce and Bentley cars, antique, classic, and contemporary. A breathtaking experience awaited us there. Standing in lead position in the showroom, gleaming, glorious and eye-shattering, was the most exquisite "Dual-Cowl" Rolls Royce (1931) Phantom II Phaeton anyone could ever expect to see on this planet. About a mile long, its chrome parts glistened and danced; the mirror-like maroon body and jet black fenders sent flashes of light in all directions, like a rotating dance-hall reflector bauble. The sensational interior was finished in creamy-soft fawn colored Connolly glove leather. The plush red carpets were magic and flying, and the burled Circassion walnut instrument panel and door sills had to have been made personally by Mr. Chippendale. We stood mesmerized by the utter perfection of the entire conglomerate effect. It belonged in a museum, that's all there was to think.

Mr. Dale approached us, beaming. "Quite a dandy, eh what!" He clapped his hands in pleasure. "This is the finest example we have ever restored, even though it is largely a 'replica'!"

My heart fell nine stories. "Replica?!!" I exclaimed. "It looks authentic in every detail." I felt betrayed, *ausgespielt,* crushed.

He patiently explained to us, sensing our disillusionment, that the original body had been rusted out in numerous places, and that the rotted wood frames had simply fallen away after the crumbling body was lifted off the chassis. All rebuilding, he said, had been meticulously engineered to reproduce the entirely new body, therefore the word "replica." The engine of course was original, but completely overhauled, along with transmission, clutch, rear axle, and springs. He went on to say that the windshield was brand new, made to authentic detail by the old master Rolls Royce craftsman, Mr. Napoleon, then over eighty. His personal escutcheon on the side of the frame bore testimony to this nostalgic fact.

It is not really a "matter of honor," and it *is* very gratifying to see a virtually new, rare classic before your eyes. This is an art in England, where skillful coachbuilders still exist to "remake" rare automobile bodies. Naturally such prodigious effort is applied only to great and singular body styles, since the cost is a bit shocking. The price tag on the majestic replica at Dale's was 8,000 pounds sterling. Translated into dollars, that's about $20,000 today. Quite a hefty figure for a "retread," as gorgeous as it may be. I mentally added shipment costs to the U.S., plus crating, insurance, custom duties, excise taxes—pushing the total to well over $22,000. Mr. Dale had mentioned that it was used as the company's lead parade car, so out of curiosity (what else?) I asked if it was for sale.

"We'd be most reluctant to sell; I don't believe we'd ever do another like it," was his reply.

At that moment, the "Radcliff Syndrome" was born, first smashing, then enveloping our senses like ozone after a lightning bolt. I looked at Bobbie, and sensed a similar stirring. She knew, as I did, that we would not buy *this* car, but she also recognized it as an ultimate collector's item to be owned, though *not* in replica form. We had both been occasionally exposed to this sticky question at shows back home, where rigid rules apply to original authenticity, and, generally, "replicas" are considered a minor abasement of the art of restoration. Often such perfect beauties do not win the First Prizes to which they seem unquestionably entitled. Despite their owner's trenchant desire to keep the fact a secret, the story inevitably leaks out that the car is a modern reproduction, and much of the competitive gloss is dimmed. (There is one famous and respected Rolls Royce collector in the South who refuses to discuss the matter, but almost everyone knows one of his greatest cars was a replica.) It was sheer delight, however, for us to browse about the heavenly Rolls, making mental notes for the future. In a hurried snatch of a conversation we had already Formally Notified Each Other of this goal—to find a Rolls Royce Phaeton of similar design; one that waited "somewhere" for restoration and our loving touch, but certainly at much lower initial cost.

There was nothing else like that Rolls anywhere in Europe that summer.

We did look and ask around for the next few weeks, hoping that some tycoon in Belgium, France, or Switzerland might have brought one over to the Continent during the intervening years, but our mild search was fruitless, and we were really not too surprised or disappointed.

Upon our return home, we were stimulated to see an announcement that the Fort Lauderdale Region of the AACA had captured the rare privilege of a "National Meet" to be held in the spring. This is the most important type of event in the car buff's world, and requires super-special planning and attention to the finest details. Winning a First Prize in a National entitles the owner to mount the aforementioned, small, enameled oval plaque on the car boasting that the car is a "National First Prize Winner." There is nothing more de rigueur that can be accomplished in the vintage motorcar world, and even the public bystanders regard this emblem with proper awe and admiration. Being so desirable, it follows that it is not easily attained. That's the way of the world, and we accepted the challenge.

Judging rules for these rigid events are quite different from regular inter-competition scoring. In the National the cars are judged "by the numbers," on 1000 points, and not basically in competitive relation to each other; a minimum of 95 percent is required for First Place. It is therefore possible (though not too probable) for more than one car in each class to be awarded the much sought-after top title and plaque, provided the runner-up scores within fifteen points of the top score Number One winner. We busily analyzed our possibilities, and came to the conclusion that the Lagonda would be our logical first choice. Fortunately, there were to be a number of prior Regional and Local Meets to put us to the acid test for the big event. The first of these "rehearsals" was at Winter Garden, Florida, on the 100-point system.

Several weeks before this show, I was invited to judge luxury "American Classics," 1929 through 1941. (There is an unwritten rule that no judge may work in his own class of car ownership, in our case "European Classics," for obvious reasons—how easy it would be to succumb to temptation and rip into a competitor's car. But who would do such a thing?)

Preparation for judging takes place on the show morning prior to the line-up of the cars. All the judges gather for discussion and coffee under the direction of the Chief Judge (no, he does not wear a white wig) to obtain the orchestration for the concert. The rules are reviewed, many admonitions are offered, and personal observations are laid out by the "C. J." In this instance, it was Dick Terhune who wore the mantle. Dick is a former aeronautical engineer who gave up his career to become a professional vintage car restorer. He was a warm and thoughtful young man, and advised us to be reasonable and courteous and "forgiving" wherever possible. I heartily endorsed this fine attitude; the six teams (usually thirty judges) then went swarming out like locusts.

Winter Haven is one of Florida's oldest inland resorts, located in the heart of the lake country. The rambling wood-frame Seminole Hotel, famed in the early 1900s for its gracious setting, had formerly been a social hub for a wealthy segment of northern society winter residents. Over the years, as the lower Florida beach coasts developed, the hotel had gradually lost its snob status, and had finally become an unrestored relic. The lawns and gardens around the lakefront, however, were kept in fine condition, and it was on this terrain that the show was held.

Judging in a large spread-out area makes it difficult for an owner-exhibitor-judge to know when his own car is being raked over; absorption with his chores sometimes causes him to miss being present at his car at the critical moment of judging. Unknown to me, the Lagonda judging was already ancient history. When I learned of this, quite upset, I hastily searched for Bobbie. She looked at me coolly, held up her hand as if to say, wait a minute, don't get excited! and told me that *she* had successfully performed all the rituals of starting the car, demonstrating lights, horn, wipers. All had gone swimmingly. I recognized then that she had become a full-fledged collector in her own right and surmised that she had charmed the judges to boot. She is better than me under that grueling, undignifying pressure.

The Lagonda scored top points in its class, a total of 96, we learned later. There is an exaggerated axiom in the car biz that every point over 90 costs $1000 to achieve. I have never agreed with this weighty rule-of-thumb, but I will admit that every point over 95 comes pretty close to this figure. However, I remembered the instructions to all judges to be "forgiving," and when Bobbie told me that Dick Terhune had been one of the judges on our car, some of the sparkle of the high score dimmed slightly. (Looking ahead to the National Meet coming up in the fall at Fort Lauderdale, we could take nothing for granted, and we realized that the treatment there would be coldly impersonal, more rigid, and highly demanding.)

After the competition period, all the cars were reassembled for public viewing in the park, downtown in Winter Haven. As we strolled along the sidewalk bordering the display area, our attention was caught by a lovely, graceful, black 1939 BMW "327" convertible. It was parked at the curb with the devil's "For Sale" sign in the window. A fair-sized group of people were poking about and talking to the owner. He explained to us that he had bought the car in Germany while on military duty, and that it was in original condition. It obviously needed some work mechanically, and a general uplift of body, paint, and chrome. The interior leather and instruments were in fine shape. With a new set of tires, new carpets, and a general tuning, I felt she would make a nice daily-use classic. We took a few turns around the park in the BMW; she handled excellently with typical German cornering characteristics. Starting her up was a slow grind, but the owner assured us that he had a crate of spare parts, including a rebuilt Bosch starter.

We made our offer, about 25 percent lower than his asking price. The owner said there were two other interested prospects, and that he'd let us know that evening after the awards banquet. Setting a price on a relatively little-seen marque like the classic BMW is almost pure guesswork; the seller usually has a figure in his mind which represents his base cost, plus whatever profit the deal will bear. The first play having been made, we agreed to meet that evening.

Later, we found him in deep discussion with two other collectors whom we recognized immediately. I thought I'd better make my next move fast, and sauntered over casually to join the group. All conversation stopped, and to my surprise the others drifted away with some mumbling about seeing him later. This was my clue that they hadn't made any firm offers. I repeated my earlier offer. We haggled awhile, and he attempted to upgrade me, hinting that he'd had a better offer. I raised my bid about 10 percent. He knitted his brow for my benefit, and said he'd let me know in half an hour. A

Sporty looks and sweeping lines of the charming 1939 BMW "327" Convertible Cabriolet, showing new black-and-cream paint job.

few minutes later I saw him earnestly conversing with another car collector from Palm Beach.

Bobbie and I sat imperturbably in the lobby, gauging the final result. He watched us out of the corner of his eye. We waited for the game to run its course. In a few minutes he approached us, hand outstretched, and said, "She's yours!" The limited auction was over.

The BMW was delivered to our home the following week, and I eagerly drove it to my office the very next day. It was a splashy, rainy day, and not a fair tryout. Every old car has its peculiarities, but the BMW threw a new wrinkle at me. A strange stench filled the car; mysteriously it stank of a stable, and I idly wondered if it had ever been stored in a barn near horses. This was certainly not a desirable condition. I also discovered that when the weather was dry the stench disappeared—the only time it happened was during a steady rain. So we started pulling things apart, lifted carpets, dragged out the seats, sniffed around underneath and even in the engine compartment. The mystery remained doggedly unsolved. I tried to use the BMW in good weather only, but it still bugged me. We went ahead with the cosmetic work, rechroming and refinishing. A thorough engine tune-up and starter replacement made the car a pleasure to drive.

Rear view of the BMW with the unique molded-in continental spare wheel detail and contoured rear deck, with wrap-around bumper.

One morning I left home in our typically beautiful Florida sunshine; returning that evening I ran into a heavy tropical downpour. The horsey smell became intolerable. It was mandatory that the mystery be solved! Again we tore apart the interior, this time removing door panels, pulling leather off the seats, separating the seat padding, but still no solution appeared. What a ridiculous dilemma. Do you get rid of a car because it smells in the rain? Maybe I had to keep a gas mask in the glove compartment.

We decided to go ahead anyway and restore for show, going at least as far as possible toward Third Place points. Among other things this required a new canvas top installation. To our surprise and delight the new top solved the mystery. Our upholsterer told us that the old mohair fabric top was originally made with horsehair; after aging for many years the hair fabric reverted to its natural state. I had been riding a wet, sweaty horse!

POSTSCRIPTS BY MY WIFE

For awhile, during a lull in the patient, slow search pattern for the Rolls, my unswervable husband seemed *to be fairly satisfied with his new Daily Use Classic, the BMW. I too liked her stubby European looks, although I could never drive her comfortably. The long flexible floor shift stick never found the right channel on the first try, and reverse was a real struggle for me. I used to complain to Alan, and he'd slide in and make me feel foolish with a slick-as-a-whistle-drop into the backing slot. Huh. Superior Men! And oh, yes, did that horsey smell ever knock out my sinuses!*

Otherwise, she was a sweet running little baby, with a nice back seat for the usual impedimenta of the family. We had a lot of starter trouble, even with a spare, and I once got so sore at the chugging and grinding, I almost furiously pushed the starter button right through the dashboard.

When we repainted her black and cream, and put that nice new black hat on her I felt like I'd been on a shopping spree at Bergdoff's and had come home with a new flossy ensemble.

How come I get so involved?

7

She Done Me In!

Our next big project was to start the Bentley on the check-out for the National Meet as Car No. 2. We decided to take a preview judging and trailered her upstate about 60 miles for a show sponsored by the Vintage Car Club of the Palm Beaches. Our trailer had been reworked by stiffening the frame and adding truss bars to both side panels. We hoped this would give us a more stable and dependable ride. Having learned our lesson well with this trailer, we slowly wound our way up U.S. 1, and arrived late due to heavy Saturday morning traffic. All the cars were lined up for judging, and we had to park in an area some distance away from our class, adjacent to the Fords and other small cars. A little, gentle, gray-haired lady came up with a stunner of a question.

"What year Ford is this?" she asked innocently. Who could really blame her? But the racey Bentley quivered in pain.

We privately and expertly pre-judged our competition, and advised the judges where to find the out-of-position Bentley. Our own objective scoring hopefully indicated that we were tops in our class of nine cars. We were right! The Bentley took First Place. She too had now earned her cups, and though not pointing as high as the Lagonda, she moved into our growing Winner's Circle.

Preparations for the big National Meet continued actively on both cars. We spent weeks anaylzing the Iron Duke, so named because of the Lagonda's battleship gray color, but perhaps also as a result of Jack Bond's comment that all Americans thought the big luxury English cars had sometime or other belonged to a "Dook." Notes were made of every minute discrepancy we could unearth, and we started working on the really hard to find point pickups. In order to check our paint job thoroughly, we decided to get a professional compounding first, which usually discloses fine cracks and "crows' feet" not otherwise discernible. It was arranged that Bobbie would follow behind me in the Buick Riviera on the way to the polisher's, to protect the Lagonda from any possible rear-end mishaps in traffic. Ordinarily this would be quite absurd, but we were taking no chances. We also had a small local show scheduled within two weeks, and looked forward to another First Prize for the trophy room.

On the way over to the body shop where the cleanup was to be done, I had to stop for gas. Bobbie followed me very carefully, staying well behind. I paid the gas ticket and started down the station ramp to the street, pausing cautiously to wait for a clear opening to enter the traffic lane. Suddenly I felt a heavy, jolting smack in the rear. *Unbelievably,* my own Riviera showed in the rearview mirror—I had been hit by my own car, by my own wife!

My response to this incredible debacle was pure reflex. I literally flew out of the Lagonda. Bobbie sat horrified in the Riviera, stunned by the exquisite irony and improbability of this accident. Her front end had charged over the Lagonda bumper, smashed into the rear deck and the right rear fender, taking with it the taillight, trunk handle, tailpipe, and lower fittings. As we were now blocking taffic on the street—the Lagonda had lurched forward about 5 feet—I yelled for her to back up to release me, and then follow me down the street where we could pull over to the curb to assess the full extent of the damage.

The beautiful and wild hilarity of this Keystone Cop farce had not yet reached my exploding conscious mind, which at that moment was swirling red, purple, and black. I could only think between gasps that she had better have a beaut of an explanation! (Tearfully, she explained later that she had looked to the left to check oncoming traffic, and assuming that I had already pulled out in front of her, she moved right on—but I was still there!) Crossing through a changing light, I blasted down the street, with a symphony of tinny, clanking noises banging in the rear. I pulled over to the curb, followed by the Buick. As though shot from a cannon, I flew out, alternately gasping for breath and blowing out exclamations like, "Omigod! It's unbelievable! " and "What a nightmare! "

I trotted from one car to the other, checking the damage, shaking my head in horror. Just then a small white pickup truck screeched to a stop behind us, and a tiny man came rushing over yelling, "Don't worry lady, I won't let him hit you!"

Glowering from my 6'2'' height, I turned on him with all my pent-up fury and shouted, "Get the hell out of here, you little jerk. That's my wife!"

He took one look at my purple Olympian majesty, scurried back into his truck, and quickly disappeared into the stream of traffic. Poor chap, he was only trying to help, having obviously seen the entire incident at the gas station. His efforts were rewarded in typical payment made to all Good Samaritans.

We stood there surveying the splendorous bust-up, not saying much, waiting for the dangerous temperature to drop. In a few minutes we regained minimal composure, enough at least to be able to look directly at each other in short darting glances. The trite saying that "love conquers all" faced its major credibility test on that busy street, and it is no less remarkable that in less than an hour we were laughing so hard, we literally wept (partly for real weeping reasons), and this proved the sometimes theory that the human mind is made of indestructible, resilient, hard rubber. (Every time we tell this tall tale, it is accompanied by gales of laughter, and it has revived many a flagging dinner party over the years.)

Our plan to get to the body shop for compounding now of course had a far more cogent aspect; we would be seeking haven for a major repair job. Try to imagine the amazement of the manager when we drove up with our freshly crumpled aluminum rear end. He looked at us in consternation. "What the devil is this?" he cried, "I thought you were coming in for a polish job!"

He heard our story disbelievingly. In this very first telling we began to see the total absurdity of the scene. This is when our first small chuckles started. He must have thought we were crazy.

A thorough examination revealed all the extra hidden bad news. The rear impact had also dislocated both doors; they were slightly sprung and out of line with the body. We then noticed that the fender had also nosed forward, causing a scraping on the tire. This was beginning to appear in a new and worsened perspective. Obviously the jolt had laced its effect along the aluminum body, and in so migrating had cracked the aged, hard, brittle paint in various places along the quarterdeck, doors, and fenders. What a fantastic hodgepodge: nothing really irreparable, but quite a cosmetic mess.

Bobbie stood by, miserably following the step-by-step mental dismantling of the great Lagonda. My heart went out to her, and I quietly suggested that she go home. I needed a platitude as well as an attitude, and came up with the following gem. "Well," I sighed philosophically, "this is our great chance to re-do the whole car for the big show, and do it right. We've been patching and filling for a long time—the Duke really deserves a brand new suit!"

She brightened up at this idea. "How about making it white," she said eagerly. "Remember those pictures we saw in England of a white Lagonda?" Boy, does she have a recovery rate!

Our excitement mounted gradually as we discussed the possibility of a complete body restoration; right down to the bare metal, primed and shot with twenty coats of lacquer. The body man thought it would take about three months, so that gave us a good margin for the "National." We left for home in the Riviera, cheered by this strange turn of events, forgetting completely that the Buick had a caved-in front end!

In the next week we had two more meetings at the body shop working out methods, color, and costs. We brought with us a copy of the Lagonda Club publication which showed two white cars, which were truly glittering, and rather lordly. Since the photos were captioned as First Prize winners, we felt secure about authenticity. The Iron Duke was then assigned to a private paint booth, to remain there until completed.

Within the first month the car was disassembled and stripped to the side frames, with only the quarter panels and upholstered leather interior remaining on the chassis. No half-measures were considered. At the same time the massive radiator shell and grille were removed for rechroming, along with a batch of other small items that had begun to show tiny pit marks. With the body vivesected, we had a good opportunity to catch up on numerous other point-gainers, and greedily decided to garner them all.

But trouble was already on the way as the weeks painfully dragged into months. Three men sporadically worked on the car, together and separately. One young chap was an artist with the spray gun, and fortunately for us he became involved with the job as a personal labor of love. Without his unflagging devotion, spurred by several handsome gratuities, we might never have made it to the show. As time slipped away, we learned to our dismay that his boss was a bit of a tippler (which may be any man's private business, but when this goes on during the working day, at my expense, it's quite another matter). We were forced thereafter to take over the management of the work, and our alarm increased as the weeks rolled by. There was no

After the Lagonda debacle: removal of doors, fenders, running boards.

choice; again we had to participate in the restoration. Memories of the Alvis episode haunted our sleep, and the specter of missing the rare National Meet hounded us constantly.

We finally somehow reached the four-month-point in time, with all major sections rebuilt and beautifully lacquered, rubbed out, polished, and ready for final reassembly to the body. This last part of the job would have to be supervised by the manager, as he was an acknowledged metal-fitting master. Anticipating the worst, I bore down with heavy pressure and received his solemn promise that he would speed up the tempo on the reassembly. Fenders, doors, bonnet, bumpers, and chrome started to reappear in place, and it seemed like we'd make the deadline with about a week to spare.

The following Monday the boss didn't show up at the shop. No one had heard from him; there was no answer at his home phone. Our awful premonition swelled like a wet sponge into a familiar and sickening feeling of quiet desperation. Big party weekend? Bobbie then noticed that the wire spoke wheels had been covered with tarpaulins and completely forgotten in a corner, during all the pell-mell activity. All the wheels were supposed to have

The Lagonda partially disassembled and wrapped with paper in preparation for complete refinishing.

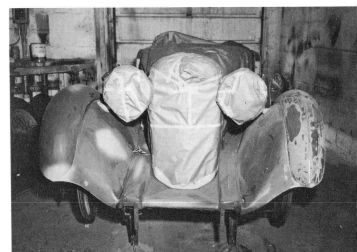

been sandblasted clean to the metal, and repainted carefully. About a month earlier, we had bought a full set of beautiful wide whitewall tires, but without refinished wheels what good were they? On a crisis-crash basis we piled the five wheels into the trunk and back seat of the Buick and rushed them over to a sandblaster for special one-day service.

Doing the best we could in our anxiety, we worked nights with the two faithful shop men, and attained a further plateau, with two weeks remaining, where the bulk of the Lagonda was refitted in quite dazzling condition. However, one major problem none of us could solve was the refitting of the front bumper to line up perfectly to the mounting brackets. Apparently when the impact had pushed the fenders forward, a mild geometric change in position had occurred, and extensive machining of the bumper support blocks was necessary. This type of heavy work was the manager's specialty, and the other chaps were in a complete sweat about where to begin.

We began to hunt feverishly. Intensive confidential inquiries finally revealed that he might be back in another day or two. The five wheels were still unpainted. That job also required his special knowledge and technique, rotating the wheels on a spindle while the paint was sprayed on evenly and slowly.

Nine days before the show we received the joyous word that the master was back on the job. Without daring a word of criticism, we joined the crew on an almost nightly basis. He said nothing, we said nothing.

The rugged job of reshaping the heavy front irons was begun: grinding, filing, and hammering until ultimately the bumper happily slipped onto its bolts. With this major headache behind us, one of the men, ticking off the checklist, noticed that we had forgotten to unwrap the paper-taped cockpit to refinish the mahogany instrument panel! We started on this painstaking job the Tuesday night before the show, at the same time they got busy on the wheels. With days and even hours now at a premium, drying periods between coats were cut short, and to top it off, it rained, retarding drying for one full day. The finished wheels therefore left quite a bit to be desired. It was now too late to argue or worry about this, and we plunged on blindly. We then had to find a tire shop willing to mount the giant new 650x18'' tires, without marring or scratching the new lacquer or scuffing the new whitewalls. This was finally accomplished on a bonus-paid basis, with the tires laid face down on clean blankets, and the wheels mounted from the rear side, taking care to cover the tips of the tire irons with taped-on protective cloth coverings to prevent scratching. Friday we spent the entire day checking all

The ugly duckling becomes a white swan.

details for the tenth time. It was hard to believe, but *five full months* had elapsed since the notorious day of the rear end collision. Our nerves (as usual) were threadbare from tension and frustration, but at five P.M. on the day *before the show,* we lovingly eased the magnificent white Lagonda out of the garage and drove it home as though we were carrying nitroglycerine in glass jars!

POSTSCRIPTS BY MY WIFE

Boy, did I pay back, and pay back, and pay back for my smashing up the rear end of the great Lagonda!

SHE DONE ME IN! / 83

After we decided to go all the way on the rebuild of the Duke, we also determined not to get caught short like we'd been on the Alvis. As the body shop men removed chrome parts, nuts and bolts, door and frame fittings and screws from inside and out, it fell upon me to be the labeler and keeper. Fair enough. This time we'd know which piece went where! Believe it or not, screws and parts that look exactly alike don't fit back into any other hole or position but the very same ones they came out of. That's because some of them were handmade to begin with. Then when you rechrome, they "grow" and change shape, so you have even more hair-raising frustrations. I always kept all my little jars and bottles from the pantry for separating the dear little goodies, and it was a mortal sin ever to throw away a coffee can.

As the job dragged on I saw that some owner motivation was called for before it was too late to do any good. At least we were in friendly territory in this particular shop. Out came my old blue jeans and I got to work, aided I suppose by a lumpy feeling of guilt and the knowledge that I'd better keep disaster at bay. The engine had been completely rebuilt in England so I didn't want to remove any of the accessories and parts that dot the engine block. Better to paint around them, I decided, so I raided Alan's oil paint art box for long sable brushes. When I get going with my sable brushes, watch out—you can't tell the result from a spray job.

The undercarriage had been steam cleaned and scraped the year before, but she still needed some refreshing and touch-up work. I borrowed a rolling dolly and spent the next few days flat on my back with spray cans and big paint brushes cleaning up this important point category. It's a good thing Grandma was visiting with us at the time—I forgot the house and kids existed. I guess it's that creative genius in me, can't mix cooking with art.

The next week, after a restoration at the beauty parlor, all dressed up for a luncheon party in silk suit, big hat, and clicking high heels, I stopped by to check on the car, though my real motive was to show those guys that I didn't always go around looking like an urchin, with black paint and grease on my face and elbows. The whoops and whistles proved I hadn't lost my feminine touch, even though I stooped to conquer—cars, that is.

8

Judged by the Establishment

The day of the long-awaited National antique and classic car show dawned mild and clear, a typical Florida October day, with a hint and a promise of cooler weather on the way. The Bentley was driven up on the trailer by a friend; I drove the immaculate Lagonda, warding off evil with rabbit's foot caution on the brake pedal. We somehow missed the show grounds in Fort Lauderdale's Lockhart Stadium after taking a wrong turn and nervously retraced our route somewhat, but the reward of seeing all the gleaming cars lined up for the great competition quickly made up for this small vexation. I mused that a double field of entries in the hot sun would make the judges short-tempered, and this could exaggerate the dangers of critical downpointing (grouchiness can cost points).

After placing both cars in their proper positions, we strolled about the grounds, leaving our older son to guard the Iron Duke and the younger with the Bentley.

Judging was about to begin. We alertly noticed that His Lordship, the Head Judge of the meet, was approaching the Bentley with his judging panel. The national reputation of this man had preceded him and there was much buzzing and comment among the collectors. "Watch out, he's a tough one"; "He's a stickler for details"; He'll tear a car apart nut by nut"; "Stay out of his way"; and other similar scuttlebutt that sounded to me like the fluttering of old ladies at a garden tea party. With uneasy thoughts, I approached the car with negatively preconditioned feelings and introduced myself. I offered the usual remarks and amenities about helping in any way possible.

Without even a nod of greeting, whammo! right off the bat, he attacked. "Whaddya mean chroming a 1924 car!" he thundered.

Set back on my heels by the unannounced onslaught, I could feel a red flush creeping up the back of my neck. I tried to control myself, and replied defensively, "I was told by experts in England that chrome appeared experimentally in 1924."

He cut me off. "Nuts!" he yelled, "there was no chrome anywhere on earth until 1926. This car is disqualified for judging!"

Anything so extreme as disqualification for one single category on the judging sheet was unheard of at meets we had attended for years. I tried to reason with him, asking that he judge the rest of the car, eliminating the points for the plating category only. I kept talking and remonstrating, trying to persuade him to be fair.

"Nothing doing!" he shouted. "This car remains *out, it will not be judged!*"

"Dammit," I replied angrily, figuring there was nothing left to lose. "What gives you the right to make that sweeping decision? You're being vindictive because I questioned your opinion. Are you judging the car, or its owner?" Attracted by the fuss, a small crowd had gathered. Bobbie ran up, tugged at my arm, and drew me aside forcibly. "Alan," she said logically, "if you let this go on he'll kill us when he gets to the Lagonda!"

That cooled me off like an ice water plunge. I had momentarily forgotten that our main objective in this show was to score top points with the Lagonda! I love all my "rolling children," each for their own special reasons; the dumping of the Bentley had totally blocked out the real goal of the day. Still I could scarcely believe that any chief judge would carry his ire from one car to another, but weighing all the dangerous possibilities I grudgingly agreed to back off. "It's sickening," I muttered as I strode away. Fortunately, we didn't have to endure that peril later, as the judging panel on the Lagonda was composed of five entirely different men.

In a few moments, we heard a commotion across the field; a crowd was gathering around a renowned 1919 Mercer owned by a highly respected collector, Elmer Rumsey from Boca Raton. The Mercer had already won a Junior National First Prize (a second National First would be termed a Senior) the previous year in a northern meet, and was considered well-nigh unbeatable, yet there glowered the Chief Judge repeating his disqualification act, for the same reason, chrome! Did you ever see a locomotive hit a solid concrete wall? There stood 5'9" David, facing 6'4" Goliath, calmly waiting for the bellowing horn to turn off. He calmly reached into his pocket, extracted his wallet, and removed a folded sheet of paper. Without a word he passed it to the vociferating Chief Judge, and stood back quietly with a little smile playing about his lips. The judge read the document, and turned several shades whiter. Without a word he irately shoved the sheet back at the owner, and ordered the panel to proceed with the judging. A cheer broke out in the crowd. What was the mysterious weapon that had subdued the giant?

I couldn't contain my impatience. As soon as the panel departed from the Mercer, I grabbed the owner's arm and propelled him away from his car.

"What the devil did you show him, Elmer?" I asked in wonderment.

He reached into his wallet again, unfolded the paper, grinning broadly. "I came prepared for that emergency," he said with a satisfied chuckle.

I read the sheet. "Vick Platers, Buffalo, New York" it read at the top of the billhead. "Platers since 1946." It went on, "This will certify that Mr. Rumsey's 1919 Mercer is completely plated with our very special industrial nickel plating, and finished to a high-chrome-like finish by a process known only to us." My glee at this turnabout was boundless. I pounded Elmer on the back as though it had been a personal victory for me. Actually, it was a victory for every collector on the field that day.

While we were chatting, we heard another donnybrook about three cars away. We raced over in time to catch the action. Lord Chief Judge was berating another collector about mismatched tires, and "what did he mean by showing up that way?"

This repeated badgering of exhibitors was unheard of in our own Regional Meets, nor have I ever seen anything to match it in any other sport or hobby, where the only intent of the participants is to enjoy the fruits of their labors, and have a little well-earned fun in the bargain.

Word reached me then that the Lagonda was next on the judging path. I hurried over in time to see one of the judges tapping on the left headlight. Bobbie was at·the light switch, pushing and twisting. "Oh no," I groaned, as the light flickered on and off. It had tested perfectly the night before. I stood there anxiously, privately damning all mechanical devices. There was our first multiple point loss! However, I hoped, with 40 points as a safety factor before we plummeted off the First Place plateau (this was a 400-point judging system; 360 were needed to stay on top) I apprehensively watched the judges work around the car, remaining at a safe distance. I was also aware that the new 400-point approach allowed the judges to chop you up into finer pieces, but I was still optimistic that the margin was balanced in our favor. That's when one of the judges crawled under the car and discovered two missing screws in the dust pan. His triumphant yell was like the knell of doom. Why, I wondered achingly, is he so damned happy about it?

Simultaneously, three other judges were on their knees before the left rear wheel. Together, Bobbie and I watched as one of them poked his finger behind the spokes, shaking his head sadly. We were getting paid off for the unavoidable rush paint job on the wheels.

There was much conferring, with all the judges in a huddle. They turned to me and said they'd be back for another go-round. This is generally considered to be auspicious as it indicates that a final score has not yet been tallied. During their short absence, we opened the headlight rim, and discovered a poor bulb connection which had apparently shaken loose on the drive up to the show. We tightened a nut—the light worked fine. The judges' second inspection was cursory, and they didn't seem overly impressed with the headlight repair. They spent a few more minutes looking at the wheels, thanked us, and walked away.

I then hunched down at the rear wheel, and found that the lacquer had "run" in two places on the hub, forming a fine snaky ridge less than an inch long. This was surely a major deduction, perhaps as much as 15 of the watered-down points. To those unfamiliar with the restoration of vintage cars, such trifles must surely seem petty and ridiculous, but these are the standards in the United States. The collector accepts them with vexation but without question. We knew then that we were a borderline case, but still half-hoped that we had not exceeded the forty-point buffer zone. There was always the possibility, too, that there would be no First Place winner at all, which could happen in any class where no car reached the 360-minimum-point level.

Like they say, "Sometimes you just can't beat the system." But we sure as hell gotta' try!

POSTSCRIPTS BY MY WIFE

Show day is also always a picnic. I mean literally.

By that I mean the best way to get food at a car show is to bring your own! After a carefully checked-out packing of polishing supplies, small parts, touch-up paint bottles and other necessary emergency equipment, I pack a large lunch with lots of drinks. Not only do I have my own four to take care of, but experience has shown me that friends and family who visit us at the shows usually happen to drift around about lunchtime. I remember one cold winter show at an orange grove where I stretched my abundant picnic basket to feed fifteen hungry mouths, even without snitching oranges. It was a good thing the main item on the menu was tuna fish sandwiches; only fish and bread could have gone that far.

The day of the big National Meet, I came equipped for quantity feeding on a hunch. The Bentley had no trunk, and the Lagonda trunk had to be shown wide open with her tools and accessories gleaming as usual. So the only place to hide the baskets and boxes and thermos jugs was under the car, sort of behind the tailpipe. Inevitably the more glamorous cars are photographed for the local newspapers. This time the photographer got a beautiful low angle shot of the car, and a great lineup of the lunch pile underneath!

The Lagonda lined up for judging at the AACA "National" in Fort Lauderdale.

Speaking of lineups, Alan had a big cheering section at this show. Typically, when Alan gets involved, everyone gets involved. That day his plant manager, his wife, and two kids were there, Alan's personal secretary, the office manager with her crew of five girls, plus some of the ladies from the packing department. Several of the factory personnel also came up with their families. They all brought their own lunches, thank goodness. In fact, someone even had a bottle of champagne to celebrate the event as well as a birthday in the crowd. Now that's loyalty for you.

When the Chief Judge disqualified the Bentley, you should have heard the howl that went up!

9

The Syndrome is Cured

 With the judging behind us, we were now on our own free time to enjoy the big National show. A nice feeling of relaxed freedom follows the competition period. That's the time you wander about and look at the other cars on display. We instinctively gravitated over to the Rolls Royce group. Eight cars stood at regimented attention, austere, proud, and radiant in the afternoon sunlight. Here was our magnet, again pulling us like moths to a flame. The elegant "Flying Lady" ornament (also known as "The Spirit of Ecstasy"), a thing of beauty in itself, perches atop that geometrically magnificent, unique, massive, blunt, beautiful radiator grille like a protective goddess, saying without words that here is the ultimate in elegance and refinement. We longingly strolled about this group of cars and paused enchanted at a Phantom I, 1930 Ascot Phaeton, slightly reminiscent of the beauty in London. From any angle she had a gorgeous body despite the incomplete restoration, lack of detailing, and rough areas in the paint, chrome, and leather. We searched out the owner, popped the question, and learned promptly that the car was not for sale.

"Really," he said politely, "we love this car. The phaeton body is rare, and very hard to find." Most of this bad news we already knew, and the Syndrome swelled with another confirmation. We resolved anew then and there to get on more seriously with the business of finding our own Rolls Royce Phaeton.

Rested and impatient, we arrived early for the pre-awards cocktail party. Congratulations for our superb Lagonda came from many of our friends, but we had to guard against presuming too much from this. The banquet followed, with the seemingly endless speeches and ceremonies. Finally that tense moment arrived: the awards announcements began. It was a blur, an endless droning until our class was called. We stiffened up, hanging on every word. Third Place was called. Second Place was called. There it was. "Alan Radcliff's 1936 Lagonda." I went up for the award, ears tingling, waiting for the First Place announcement. But there was no First—though we were Second, we were "Best in Class." No other car in our class had achieved the minimum points!

In a standard competitive meet, we would therefore have taken the top award; in the new, separated scoring system we were simply locked into the mathematics.

Stumbling miserably back to our table, I could not conceal my profound disappointment. Many handshakes were offered, and Bobbie greeted me with a little shake of her head and teary eyes. Considering the months of toil and tension we had lived through, Second Place was a slim reward indeed. I patted her hand and felt her misery keenly, despite the fact that being the Best in Class was high praise in itself. "Oh, those wheels," she sighed softly, "oh, those wheels!"

The ache, as always, subsided gradually in the next few days, the National was deliberately forgotten, and we started planning our next campaign which we jokingly entitled, "Cherchez la Rolls." I wrote to many people we knew around the country who might start the leads flowing. One of my business distributors, sort of a car buff himself in California, wrote that he knew of a Rolls Phaeton near San Francisco; he thought it was for sale. A collector friend in Chicago wrote back that there were several of them in that area too. Several other replies established that there were not too many of our specific type for sale, so we began sliding our fingers over the classified ads in borrowed copies of *Flying Lady* (published by the Rolls Royce owners club) and other publications in the field. I made a series of long distance phone calls within two months, but for one reason or another the leads petered out.

Sometime within the next half-year my business required that I make a cross-country trip to visit several of our major factory agents. I arrived first in Chicago on a Sunday morning, and was whisked out to see two cars, by appointment. One of them, a great Derby 1929 Phaeton, had been renovated for personal use, and was entirely unauthentic. I appraised it with an open mind, knowing that it was a fine body style, but at the asking price, the necessary restoration would be a long, expensive, uphill climb. I passed it by reluctantly, there was simply too much to do to make it a showpiece. The other Rolls was a 1934 Phantom II, a very boxy, nondescript job that I thought might have been originally built as a saloon (sedan). Its unprofessional-looking conversion to an open touring car had really been a waste of time I thought, recognizing that even the many vaunted Rolls Royce coachbuilders made sundry bad mistakes. With the vision of the "London Rolls" always in my mind, it was impossible to consider this rough mongrel.

After completing my meetings in Chicago, I left for San Francisco. Following a couple of days of business affairs, I drove down to my next Rolls appointment on Saturday morning. This time I saw a great example of a P.I 1928 Pall Mall Phaeton. My search could have ended here, but—not so fast! The car was part of a sizable collection, all locked in an estate settlement with probate complexities, lawyers, and claims. The theoretical price tag was over $20,000, quite unrealistic I felt, under the circumstances. True the car was almost precisely what we were looking for, but when I added transport costs from the West Coast, and considered the dangers of over-the-road shipment for over 3,500 miles, I recognized the futility of making a serious try at buying the car. Also, the estate lawyers admitted that it could be a year or more before it would be released for sale, and that clinched it. With a last nostalgic backward glance, I walked out on this fine Rolls, wondering where I'd pick up the trail next.

Later that spring, we had an important opportunity at Cypress Gardens to capture a "Senior" First Prize with the Lagonda, which is rated almost as important as a National Junior win. This means that any car returning to the same club after winning a previous First Prize in that club is automatically removed from its basic class competition, and competes with other previous Junior First Prize winners. This is not done in all clubs (would that it were!) and it permits newer restored cars to take their Junior Firsts without being blocked by their more mature, and sometimes unbeatable predecessors.

In 1965 we had taken our first Junior win at Cypress Gardens with the gray-bodied Iron Duke, and this qualified the now-white Lagonda for prestigious Senior judging. As expected, we did win the Senior award in "Classic," but we were almost blasé after our years of wins with this wonderful automobile. Our trophy room at home proudly displays a valued assortment of silver trays, cups, and bowls, as well as a multitude of vertical winged-victory trophies and wall plaques, many of them garnered by the Lagonda. It was without a doubt the winningest car we ever owned, and accounts for almost half the awards taken by the various other cars combined.

Summer vacation was at hand. Our plans were to visit Canada, where we hoped there would be a number of Rolls Royces around Montreal and Quebec. Also, a letter had recently arrived from our dealer-friend in London, Jack Bond, advising that one of his customers in Connecticut had a 1926 Pall Mall Tourer, suggesting that we go up and have a look at it. I phoned and made an appointment. We flew up to New York, rented a car, looked at a battered tourer in Westchester that had been on our list, felt sorry for the owner, and headed up to New England for the next stop in the quest. We arrived in Farmington in fog and a pouring rainstorm, drove around for a maddening hour looking for the nonexistent address, and finally stopped into a foreign car showroom to inquire. Yes, they knew the car in question, it was owned by an eccentric British metal sculptor who sometimes forgot his own address! We eventually found the place, hidden in a courtyard behind a narrow alleyway, between two ancient New England clapboard houses of the Victorian period. It was easy to see why the gentleman forgot his address, there wasn't one posted anywhere.

We bounced through the flooded ruts in the lane that unexpectedly opened into a clearing, which was jammed with welded iron sculpture of the most avant garde connotation. We slowly splashed our way through the puddles looking for someone to talk to, and almost ran into a figure approaching out of the mist. He was directly out of the pages of a Dickens' novel, surely a non-stop arrival. This reedy, strangely charming character, apparently in his sixties, sported tweed knickers, argyle socks, and Chukka boots, all topped off with a red velvet English schoolboy's skullcap, gold tassel, braid, and all. This was our sculptor.

He greeted us cordially, smiling beneath his India military mustache, his wispy, thin, gray hair peeking out beneath the cap. "Delighted to meet-chya," he said in a clipped British accent; I hoped his Rolls was as authentic as he was.

He guided us to a dilapidated, picturesque barn that looked like it had been erected as a model for artists' sketching only. Inside, it was festooned with cobwebs, crowded with farm implements, mechanical gear, and junk of all kinds. It was totally unlighted and windowless. There in the midst of this make-believe stage set squatted the "Pall Mall" Rolls, laden with saddles and

A roomful of trophies—the author and his wife showing two of their favorite car models.

blankets, piled around with harnesses, hay bales, and spare engines. I chortled quietly at this delicious tableau—it was so authentic it should only have been preconceived by Hollywood prop experts. Bobbie glanced at me carefully, a stifled laugh in her eyes. We could both already imagine the condition of the car.

Our examination was a shocker. The windshield, he admitted, was from a 1931 La Salle, fitted to the cowl by the addition of a curved sheet metal pan to fill in the gap. Flabbergasted, we continued our inspection. Evidence of his ability as a metal sculptor showed everywhere. He had over the years, made almost endless modifications to the body. Apparently, the original trunk rack hadn't pleased his aesthetic sense, so he simply cut it off and extended the body about two feet. Both the front and rear seats, what we could see under the pile of debris, had been reshaped and rebuilt with modern drop-down arm rests of Cadillac origin. The ragged upholstery showed through the dust as a faded red brocade fabric. We then extracted from him the information that the instrument panel was from a 1952 Buick (he liked the shape of it, he confided), but the greatest bafflement of all was when he lifted the bonnet, and we gaped at the battered engine from the same '52 Buick.

"What happened to the original Rolls engine?" I asked in a mild state of shock.

"Oh, that's used as a winch on my old fire engine," he retorted cheerfully.

In stupefaction Bobbie and I avoided looking at each other. Why embarrass the nice old gent; we could easily have flown into side-splitting laughter. Our controlled politeness must have somehow communicated itself to our guide, and he abruptly said, somewhat shamefacedly, "I guess you're surprised at what's been done to the Rolls. Anyhow, would you like to see the rest of my collection?"

"Certainly!" we replied thankfully—anything to get away from the gruesomely botched-up Rolls-Frankenstein!

We sloshed around the compound, looking first at his 1906 buckboard "Country Gentlemen," a wood-bodied, bicycle-wheel antique, also rebuilt much to his own unusual tastes. He then proudly showed us his pièce de résistance, an excellent 1930 dual-windscreen Packard Phaeton. This was a real car, and we perked up. He *did* know how to restore for show, and we learned that the Packard was a consistent prize winner. Next we viewed a charming, tiny, red 1903 Renault two-seater, then his La France fire engine, and finally a lithe 1932 two-seater Lagonda Rapide boattail racer. This car

Senior First Prize Winner at Cypress Gardens: the 1936 4.5 liter Lagonda, now in white

1927 Rolls Royce Phantom I Phaeton at the AACA Meet in Fort Lauderdale

was also for sale, and though we were mildly tempted to ask the price, our resolve for a Rolls was our only guideline, and we resisted. Our visit ended with an invitation to tea, served in a low-beamed, softly-lighted, woody room filled with books, art, and flowers. Our remarkable host showed us some of his small interpretive sculpture, all ingeniously and exquisitely welded together from bits and pieces of metal, wire, gears, fan blades, and pickups of every conceivable nature. Looking back, we count this short, warm visit among the most pleasurable in our years with the cars.

We drove back to New York, more disconsolate than ever about the chances of finding our Phaeton. Bobbie reminded me of a private belief we've had for years: that when the right time comes, the right things happen to us. I consoled myself with this bit of mystique. Apparently then, the right time hadn't come. So why did I feel so frustrated? No point of logic there, I told her succinctly. We picked up Bennett, our younger boy, whom we had left with my brother in New York, and flew up to Montreal the next day. We had accumulated names of several well-known collectors, partly from the Rolls Royce Owners directory, and partly from leads gathered during the year. Our first and most important call was another smashing disappointment. We were advised that an entire major collection had recently been auctioned off, including three Rolls soft top models. Where did they go, I asked. Two of them (now hear this!) had been shipped back to England, and the other wound up in Denver. Instantly, our best lead had fizzled away.

Other contacts unearthed a superlative set of "reasons why not." Owners were on vacation in Europe; one car was already on option to a Houston collector; one of them was completely stripped down for a total restoration ("Come see it next year"); and, of course, several others were not for sale.

One day, while driving on one of Montreal's wide and handsome boulevards, we spotted a beautiful Rolls tourer moving in traffic about half a block ahead of us. We were behind a taxi, which was behind a bus. Two trucks were over to the left, and we could see several cars behind the Rolls, in the adjacent lane.

Bennett, our great car aficionado and traffic adviser, shouted, "Daddy, there's a space between the trucks!"

I shot into the tight gap, while the truck driver swore at me and shook his fist like any decent self-respecting New York-type truck driver. Unexpectedly, the Rolls pulled in to the right lane and made a fast turn into a side street. Just then the light turned red, the bus pulled up to the corner blocking me, and I was prevented from making another move under threat of extinction. By then all three of us were jumping up and down in our seats with exaggerated anxiety; this had momentarily become a vital matter. It seemed an hour before the light changed. The bus and its following stream of traffic started moving, and that left me no choice but to continue straight on in my center lane. I edged over as quickly as possible into the right lane, signaling frantically, horn blasting, and made a wide right turn on two wheels into the nearest side street. Racing down to the next corner, I made another right, and then a screeching left, eyes straining to spot the Rolls again. But it was gone, gone, gone, swallowed up in the busy city traffic. Finis to that episode.

Our next wraithlike lead led us to the outskirts of Quebec City. We had been promised in Montreal that there was a commercial garage near Quebec, jam-full of great classics in fine condition, but beyond that narrow description, no specific facts were known. The address proved accurate; a gasoline station complex with an adjacent used car lot and two large sheds in the rear, enticingly padlocked. An elderly gentleman greeted us spouting French patois, which didn't ring a bell in our limited and rusty language belfry. We stared at each other in that typical bewilderment and embarrassment caused by the language barrier, until we were saved by the driver of a truck who had just pulled in for gas. Our interpreter advised us that the "son-in-law" was out to lunch, but that he could be phoned at home. We rang him up. He said he had two phaetons in the shed, but his only Rolls Royce was a 4-door saloon. We decided to wait and see the cars anyway. This proved to be extremely worthwhile; all the cars were in superb condition. The Rolls, however, was another of those bulky, square 20-25's, made to order for Dracula's arrival at the Opera.

"Phooey," disdainfully said my young lover of the Rolls Royce strain, "who needs it!"

We passed on to a lovely, dark blue 1926 Lincoln 4-door open tourer, and then to a striking 1928 maroon and black Franklin Dual-Cowl Phaeton. It was really a beauty, but who wanted a Franklin? There was also a real sporty black and tan Packard roadster in the smaller shed, and we gasped with pleasure as the garage door swung open. It was not for sale—about that one I asked! The visit was now purely academic, and we enjoyed ourselves immensely. (Moments like these help make the whole back-and-heartbreaking hobby worthwhile.) Then we saw the parts bin! Never before had we even imagined a collection of body sections and parts to equal the rich storehouse in this shed. Neatly ranged around the walls on shelves from floor to ceiling exploded an endless variety of antique fenders, doors, bumpers, windshields, springs, and engine parts of every kind, all worth a fortune. What a feast—we were in the midst of a parts treasure trove to dazzle any vintage car collector in the world! We made lists of some of the rarer items, and promised to pass the information to our clubs in Florida.

We spent the next five days in Quebec City, vacationing and sightseeing. As usual we made some inquiries, and were told that there were no known Rolls Royce Phaetons around that area, but that there were probably several in the Toronto area. That was quite a westward haul, and we promptly quashed that possibility.

The final swing on our trip took us up to Gray Rocks Inn in the Laurentian Mountains. This was to be *pure* vacation, we said. So we promptly checked possibilities with the hotel manager. He seemed to remember having heard about an old Rolls somewhere in the vicinity, and promised to investigate. About two days later he rang our room and confirmed that an old lady who lived on Mt. Tremblant was reputed to own a Rolls Royce. He had unearthed a phone number. With that old tingling sense of expectancy we rang up.

A man answered, speaking French. "Parlez vous anglais?" I asked anxiously.

"No, no," he said, waiting.

There was a little pause. "Merci," I said hopelessly, having exhausted my pitch.

I contacted the manager. He pleasantly agreed to make the call for us. A few moments later he rang back. "The elderly madame is on a tour of Europe," he had been told by the butler. We felt better when he said that he had been told the Rolls was a 1939 limousine. It was pretty obvious by then why the Rolls we were seeking was called a Phantom I. Ghostly spirits indeed.

We returned to Miami from our Canadian trip, pleasantly tired, and chafing under the expanding cloud of disappointment about the Rolls search; I believe I would have traveled to India to continue the hunt at that point. Life resumed in the normal pattern, but the Syndrome remained like a sore tooth. We eagerly read the ads from cover to cover each time monthly car publications arrived. Now and then an elusive phaeton appeared in a classified ad, but by the time we called, it was either sold, or it was the wrong type, or the price was too high.

We continued to write to the British dealers. Jack Bond responded that he was dickering for a 1926-dual-cowl phaeton, and if he could make the deal, he would start a total restoration, and probably have it ready by the following summer. He quoted a round figure of about $16,000—more or less the same old ritual price. We put an ice pack on the tender tooth, and tried to forget about it for awhile.

In the fall of 1968, a bright red 1957 Jaguar XK-140 joined our collection. While this was not in the show sense a classic car, I felt Bobbie would enjoy driving it. It handled beautifully, and the paint, chrome, leather, and top were in excellent condition. A new set of wide whitewall tires made it a sharp looking little bomb, and it diverted our attention for awhile. Bobbie was thrilled. She had never had a true sports car before, and though it was not in the competition category, it was a worthy example for any car lover. This now brought us up to four cars in the collection, plus the station wagon and the Riviera. With enclosed storage space for three, our front courtyard began to look like we were always having a party.

A few months later, while reading the "Classic and Antique" car section in the Sunday *Miami Herald* classified, I came upon another car with which I had always had a clandestine love affair. It was a 1952 Mercedes-Benz 300D, 4-door convertible, the massive and luxurious postwar Mercedes' answer to Rolls Royce. This car originally sold in 1952 for $18,200, and was recognized as a magnificent machine. I phoned the owner, and we rushed out to see it. The car had been beautifully restored; the engine had been completely rebuilt, new tires were fitted, and the red leather was in fine condition. The interior was huge, in the grand-touring style of the great classics, with deep bucket seats in front, and a deeply padded curved-bench seat in the rear. Leg room in the back allowed full stretch for me extended. We bought it on the spot, while three other buyers stood outside the garage anxiously waiting for us to turn it down. Probably this waiting line had something to do with our rapid decision, along with our immediate agreement to sell the station wagon in order to keep our total to six. Bobbie would now also have a classic Supermarket Special, with an enormous trunk for shopping bags, and more than enough space to carry six or seven kids to school in the neighborhood car pool program. "Pretty nice school bus," she used to say primly, with a twinkle in her eyes.

Lest you think us disloyal to an idea, these latter two additions to our covey of cars had no curative effect whatsoever on the Rolls Royce ailment.

We still smelled, felt, and dreamed Rolls Royce with fluctuating blood pressure and regular fever flareups, which cooled with each abandoned search. Our regular car show attendance continued through the winter months while we consistently racked up top-trophy wins with the Bentley and the Lagonda. We had repainted the Lagonda wheels and replaced the missing screws in the dust pan. This was now a pretty hard car to beat.

One day in March we unexpectedly received an incredible and electrifying bit of information. One of the local club members, visiting our home, got into a casual discussion with us about Rolls Royces. We mentioned our Rolls safari adventures over the years, embellishing each incident in the narrative. He looked at us in surprise.

"Don't you know about the '27 Rolls Phaeton that's been stored right here in Miami for about four years?"

"What Rolls are you talking about?" I shot back in astonishment.

"The "T" Rolls, that's what!" he said. "It sounds exactly like what you're looking for. As a matter of fact," he added, "I've heard it's going to be advertised in the next issue of *Hemmings* (the car buffs' marketplace) which will be out this week!"

The irony of this was almost too much to swallow. If this was really the car we had been tracking halfway around the world, how could it possibly have been sitting in our own hometown for years?

The "newest thing" in school busing–the 1952 Mercedes-Benz 300D four-door convertible sedan.

We contacted the owner at once, and heard in complete disbelief, from his description of the car, that it was a special four-door tourer, mostly restored, and located less than four miles from where we lived! It had been under wraps for years, and was now finally being offered for sale.

Early the following morning after an understandably restless night, we rocketed over to the garage and watched anxiously as the canvas cover was unrolled, exposing the long, lean, phaeton dream car. It didn't matter that the paint was chipped and dull, and that most of the chrome was pitted, or that the interior had been ridiculously reupholstered in diamond-tufted black vinyl, or that the door hinges were an abortion. What mattered was that she was a 1927 Rolls Royce P-I Phaeton, all there and in running condition, and wondrously waiting to be bought! She had the gracious and elegant low line of our First Love in London, including the magnificent 3-section chrome and glass rear seat windscreen. It was a Brewster-bodied Rolls, built in Springfield, Massachusetts, on a standard P-I chassis, one of those advance-styled great American Rolls built during almost a decade in cooperation with General Motors. She was pure Rolls Royce, with a stance like a blue-ribbon Great Dane. It was almost too much to absorb—we were ecstatic. To think of all the places we had gone to find her, we kept repeating to each other, while she was sitting right here in Miami! Allowing for several thousand dollars for complete restoration, this could be the end of our search.

We still had a major hurdle to vault over. Having just placed his ad at an admittedly high price, the owner wanted to wait until his inquiries started to arrive. I knew that I had to negotiate at once. I made what I considered to be a realistic offer. He considered it doubtfully.

"I think I'd better wait until I see how the ad pulls," he said slowly. "Who knows, I might get my full asking price." Somehow this had to be avoided.

I had a flash of inspiration, remembering from previous conversations we had had with each other at car shows, that he had always liked my 3-liter Bentley: he had eyed it more than once with an open interest. It was obviously better suited to his small build than to my big one—and conversely the 19-foot Rolls Phaeton really needed a big man with shoulders to handle its heavy steering and sheer mass. The idea of arranging a trade intrigued him, I could see that at once, and he recognized as well that the Bentley was fully restored, and had an impressive record as a prize winner. The following day he came to my home, drove the Bentley, and fell in love with the irresistible features of this lovely automobile. We knew we had the beginning

The day the syndrome ended: 1927 Rolls Royce Phantom I Phaeton as she looked outside the seller's garage, before the dickering started.

of a deal working, despite the fact that he had already received two long-distance phone calls from early birds who had obtained advance airmail copies of the magazine containing the ad. He agreed that the irony of my discovering his Rolls simultaneously with the placement of his ad, after the car had been in dead storage four years was pretty hard to contemplate. At that moment, I had to live with the fantasy that the whole world was going to be bidding against me—a psychology which did not escape his notice.

No decision was made that day, although we discussed and theorized about it for over an hour. We did have a general swap formula set up, and I had agreed that the Rolls, even in her flabby and somewhat tired condition, did have a bit more basic value than the beautiful, award-winning Bentley. I followed up quickly the next morning with an additional and respectable amount of cash as a topper. He asked for time to consider. He phoned back that evening. "Still not enough," he said coyly. "By the way, I have a collector coming down from New York day after tomorrow." All's fair in this fast-paced poker game, and I realized I couldn't take the gamble on his face-down card.

I rapped out, "Okay, Okay! I'll throw in my custom-trailer," knowing for sure this would be too much to resist. I was right.

"You've got a deal!" he replied with obvious satisfaction. At that moment I felt he'd gotten the better end of the transaction, but I didn't care. After all, we'd found the cure for the Syndrome, and thereby eliminated the toothache forever.

POSTSCRIPTS BY MY WIFE

Yes, the Lagonda Senior First Place at Cypress Gardens was easy, but Alan didn't mention the other trophy we won! The Hard Luck Trophy. That wasn't so easy. The silver cocktail mixer engraved "Hard Luck" is standing reminder of this series of events which almost had us knocked out on two counts before we even got to the show.

The night before we were to drive up, we went over our regular checklist. Right at the top it says: Start The Engine. So we started the engine, but nothing happened. After depleting our entire stock-in-trade of standard remedies, we called in desperation on a neighbor who was a whiz with engines. This was about 9:00 P.M. A quick diagnosis showed the magneto was in trouble, not a minor problem! He and Alan pulled it out; it needed cleaning and brush remaking, and they worked on it until 2:00 A.M., and then, okay, we started the engine. Typical, no?

Friday noon we left happily on our 220 mile trip, but as we drove up the Sunshine Parkway, Alan suddenly remembered that we hadn't checked the oil level. We were coming up to a service plaza, so he slowed down and rolled into the entry lane. About 300 yards from the gas station, as we drove in the entry road, there was a loud popping noise. Blooey! We had a flat. It was a good thing we had decided to stop, otherwise it would have happened to us at high speed somewhere out on the turnpike. This was the livin' end!

When we redid the Lagonda in the fall, we had put on four brand new, expensive, custom, 6-ply whitewall tires (how could a flat have happened?) but the spare under the tire-well cover didn't match for show purposes. Alan had also had a terrible time in Miami finding the special tubes for those big 18" Denmans, and we had no extra tube with us. He sadly trudged up to the station to get us towed so we could install the spare, and then, probably go home. The White Duke didn't stand a chance for First with a mismatched blackwall tire on the front left wheel, and we weren't in the mood to drive all that way for anything less.

Fifteen minutes later he was back on the runningboard of a truck, whooping and hollering. On a wild chance (about 1,000-to-1 odds) he had asked the attendant if he had any 18" tubes, and miraculously there were two of them stuck away on a high shelf, truck size! So what if the valve was too long? What a stroke of luck. We took the extra one too. When Alan got up and told our story at the banquet, no one else could top it. So our Hard Luck helped with a little Good Luck.

Martinis made in that particular bowl always somehow taste a little better.

The Quest for the Holy Rolls, had certainly led us far afield—wide ranging and starry-eyed. That beauty in London haunted us continually. Under the heading "Now That We Knew What We Wanted," no out-of-the-way place would have been too far out of the way. It's the truth, Alan once did consider a trip to India if all else failed (the home of the Rajah Rollses). He even asked his brother, on a trip through Africa, to keep his eye peeled for her!

But to find her right here in Miami was absolutely too much to believe. We both stood transfixed when the cover was unrolled, and my own feelings surely matched the jubilation of us women suffragettes when we finally got the vote. I literally jumped up and down on my French heels!

10

Prepping the Grand Old Lady

 What a day that was, the homecoming of the long-sought-after Rolls Royce Phaeton. I quickly discovered two unhappy facts about my already beloved Rolls: first, that she was a balky starter and a sputterer on the road, and second, that the front seat must have been built for a Lilliputian chauffeur. Nothing mattered, I was on heavenly wings, borne aloft by my 7" Flying Lady ornament seemingly 10 feet out in front of me on the radiator shell. "Whatever Rola wants, Rola gets," I hummed to myself joyously in my crunched up driver's seat. Routine mechanical repairs were expected in any good high-priced purchase, and I had been assured by the seller that the engine had been completely rebuilt by an expert a few years back (at a cost of $1,100) with only several hundreds of miles run since the overhaul. This indicated that our restoration was to be mainly "cosmetic" in all departments. As for the front seat, I had previously noted that the divider panel between front and rear compartments was about 9" wide, and I confidently presumed that a reduction to 4" could be made to the oak frames, beneath the padding and leather, which would give me the needed legroom.

Our delight in performing research chores beckoned us through volumes of data in preparation for the restoration of our Rolls. Luckily, when the vinyl upholstery had been installed, several small patches of the original black leather were carelessly left under the seat frames, and we pounced on these with glee. I mailed off small cuttings to a number of New York leather dealers in Nassau Street, and was quickly rewarded with the information that the original hides were Yugoslavian calf. We assumed that Brewster specified this material, so nothing else would do. It took many weeks to locate a source for this rare item, a rich, thick, pebble-grained leather like no other, and our order was placed with a bill-of-fare of red tape and the usual obstacles. All the standard frustrations were overcome one-by-one—we wanted the real thing—and finally our 10 hides arrived for Phase I, Phantom I.

Some comments about procedure, at this point. A complete restoration usually starts with mechanical items, but since this was largely history on the Rolls, the next step was the interior. It is understandably suicidal to work the upholstery *after* the paint work is finished, as the softwork requires the workers to have constant physical contact with the body exterior. The best rule is to do the paint last, after which the chrome is cautiously reinstalled, and the car stands ready for competition. In actual fact, there is always the last detailing by the owner; the small nonsense that no commercial shop is willing to do at any price.

We therefore proceeded with George on our custom upholstery work, laying out the luscious Yugo skins, measuring, chalk-marking, planning every cut to avoid fatty wrinkles, nicks and rough spots. Only the perfect sections were to be used. Even the best hides in the world have their share of abrasions, barbed wire cuts, and even dull spots from the tannery process. Careless selection can end up with point losses, although a conscientious trimmer is aware of these pitfalls. We consulted and agreed that the pleats would be 3" wide, which was supported by evidence in photos found by Bobbie. We tore out the old door panels, and shaped new ones of rigid fiberboard in preparation for the new leather coverings. Endless conferences took place about the shape, size, and position of two flap pockets for the rear compartment partition wall. When all this was done and recorded, we started searching for a cabinetmaker to cut back the wood thickness of the divider panel to allow ample space in the front seat. The car went to him first, gently squeezed into his tiny shop between a huge breakfront and a library wall that he was building for a new lawyers' office.

After two weeks of typical frustration, diplomacy, and entreaties, the woodwork job was done (at twice the estimated figure), and we happily drove the Rolls back to the upholstery shop. We had good luck, in the final result, the gain in front seat space was 5". Why, you may ask, did they build these giant motorcars with tight front seats? The amusing fact is that all that mattered apparently was that there was plenty of legroom in the passenger area, and the chauffeur be damned. A bit of memorabilia in this connection: help-wanted ads for drivers ran something like this: "Small but strong-armed, experienced chauffeur needed for touring Rolls Royce. Hands large enough to work with big tools. Ex-jockeys may apply."

We started the major leather project, concurrently with removal of almost all the chrome parts. Our next step was to find and reserve time with a reliable master painter—no thought was given to returning to either of the previous shops! Several interviews left us hanging; the haunted house of painters held the same old terrors for us, even though we had slept there before and had come out alive, but barely. The previous relationships with car painters had not only used up our credibility; our trusting natures on that point were permanently discarded on a junk heap of bitter memories. Finally, after more than a week of visits and conversations with painters, we located in Coral Gables a "Little Old Car Painter" like the "Little Old Winemaker," who was alleged to be a master with the old-fashioned methods and cellulose lacquer finishing. He was still going strong at age 72, and though this gave me some small misgivings, the obvious benefits of his years of experience outweighed the possible peril or jeopardy. He certainly knew his business, we could see that quickly, and we made our deal for 20 coats in an authentic color combination of black and fawn. The fenders, the cowl, and half of the side panels going back to the rear doors were to be in black; from there and around the rear body behind the trunk was to be in fawn. Wheels also were to be fawn, with red drums behind the wire spokes. This promised to be spectacular, as eventually it was.

Our special Phaeton has one of the most coveted features in a Rolls Royce, i.e., a gleaming, polished satin-aluminum bonnet, replete with the sparkling rivets along the linear hinges. This graceful section is almost heart-meltingly lovely in its narrow, kingly length. The hood glistens in the sunlight like the wings of an airplane in flight. It is lovingly polished before every show, a task that is put off until last, until no further excuses can be found. It's a real dog-day program, but the end result is worth all the recalcitrant slavery. As a source of price, it is unmatched by any other feature of the car.

Things went well, as always, with George at "Custom Auto Upholstery." Of all our suppliers he is the most reliable and meticulous, albeit not a man to be pushed or easily criticized. He knows what he's doing, and the best results are obtained with friendly patience. Smoothly, by the end of January, our pungent, brand-new-smelling leather job was done. Crisp and plump, with a luminous sheen, it quite clearly forecast our high-level restoration goal. We said at the time, if all the other major projects matched it, we should have one of the finest Vintage Rolls Royces in the United States. But there was still a long way to go; with many hidden surprises tucked away here and there throughout the car.

We then decided to have an intermediate shot at the carburetion and starting problems, before going to the paint shop. Somewhere in the major engine rebuild in 1967 this mechanical area did not receive full attention, and we were determined, if possible, to eliminate the difficulty early in the agendum. Some improvement was attained at a local old-timer mechanical shop, but time was to prove that more intensive carburetor and ignition surgery would be needed later.

The next step was the fearful one, so aptly described in reverse, "Watch out for that first step, it's a bitch!" except that here we would be dealing with almost the last step: the body and undercarriage and the dressing up of the engine compartment to keynote the overall excellence. Like a dreaded visit to the dentist, when the appointed day arrives, you go. So we went to the paint shop. Conditions were different this time; we had no private stall for the Rolls, as we had for the Lagonda. We left her parked in a lineup, single file, one car in front, another car behind. The leather interior had been completely plastic covered and taped securely, as well as the doors, which were to be removed during the body prep period. The painter had agreed to strip the old layers-upon-layers of lacquer down to the metal wherever necessary, and this proved to be more, than less, as the job progressed. In 43 years a plethora of paint had been applied to our venerable Rolls Royce, and sooner or later it had to be removed, like thick varnish on a boat deck.

Our bustly and friendly septuagenarian painter tackled the job with gusto, though not starting until ten days had slipped by while he finished other work in the shop. We had allowed for this sort of time pilferage; experience having made us wiser. Also, there had been one other quotation, in the idiotic amount of $1,800 for the job, and we were able to feel tolerant, having pinned down a bid of about one-half that figure for the same specifications. This included the aforementioned strip-down; repair or welding of all metal cracks, particularly in the aluminum sections; patching and filling to eliminate every possible side-angle light ripple; and rerolling of all the fender beads. Sealing, bonding, and priming were to be done with the finest materials available, and the final lacquer was to be Ditzler or equivalent. We reduced all this, and more, to a memo that looked like a Harvard Outline for the Theory of Relativity, and departed, satisfied to the bottom of our feet. Our painter asked for the first month with no interference, to which we agreed, on a total three months schedule.

Meanwhile, all was well in the Radcliff garage. No major shows on the list; we were going to take it easy this year. Quite unexpectedly I found myself swept up in a friendly argument in our local AACA club about the advisability, or even the possibility, of preparing a show for the spring calendar. There was a half-hearted desire on the part of some of the members to have a fill-in meet as a result of a lost commitment for a major show early the following year. Usually these complicated events require a year or so of preparation—though I honestly never knew why. It's more habit than fact that it can't be done in less time. The majority of the membership was solidly against a "rush job," as one of our peers put it, and the vacillation was annoying to behold. I took the torch, largely through my nature, which urges me on when others say die. Against a mainstream of negativism, I proposed a possible solution that started a real rhubarb. The main problem was that car clubs require financial sponsorship to stage a show, either through public or private sources. Such sponsorship includes availability of capacious show grounds at no cost to the car club, donation of trophies, all or part, plus, to attract the public, advertising, printing of promotional, entry, and registration mailings, and other services not easily obtained. The benefit to a public sponsor should be commercially obvious; the show draws crowds and creates desirable publicity. Generally, therefore, these exhibitions are preferably held at tourist attractions, hotel grounds, racetracks, big shopping plazas, public museums, and the like.

My idea was to try something entirely new. I offered to contact the management, friends of mine, at the Kings Bay Yacht and Country Club located on Biscayne Bay south of Coral Gables, in an attempt to set it up for the end of May, only a few months hence. This was an unheard of tight-rope schedule; there was a hue and cry, "Impossible." "It's never been done so fast," "It can't be done!" and so on. The resistance only strengthened my determination to prove it *could* be done.

Step-by-step, I outlined the timing of preparations, and eventually won over enough members to put it to a vote. Grudgingly, by a narrow margin, they gave me the green light to make the attempt. It was not a very encouraging endorsement.

The president of Kings Bay grabbed the idea with zest, feeling it would make a unique weekend event for his club members. It was then more or less routine to engineer the details with the manager. He too felt that an Antique Car Show on the beautiful club grounds had great appeal, and promised to go all out in the sponsorship.

So there we were with a rush deadline facing us. A committee was appointed, announcement letters were printed within one week, and mailings were directed to all the Florida car collectors, numbering over 1,000. Since the announcement was printed on Kings Bay brochures, the sponsors already had their first reward for their efforts, as they reached a large mass of top-class people around the state with their own colorful promotion brochure. The car club asked me to handle the design and purchase of the trophies (under Kings Bay auspices), and this gave me an opportunity to flex my creative ideas.

Instead of the usual and often monotonous silver bowls and dishes, wall plaques, or formal vertical column trophies, I designed all the trophies to have a usable nonshelf purpose. The First Place award stood 12'' high, made of a mahogany slab, with an electric clock in the center and two quality writing pens mounted in the onyx base. The Second Place award was a chunk of mahogany on an onyx base made up as a lamp, and Third Place was an onyx paperweight, with one writing pen. The ubiquitous 4'' gold-metal antique car mascot was of course perched on top of all the awards. The trophy for Best of Show, I was told, was a masterpiece of extravagance, a three-foot high mahogany lamp with a large antique gold parchment rectangular lamp shade. It had an electric clock in the main panel, and two pens in the massive onyx base. This piece threw the allotted budget slightly out of whack, and the car club treasury had to pay about $30 for the lampshade ! Other than that, all expenses were borne by the country club.

All this hectic preparation on such short schedule threw another heavy burden upon us to finish the Rolls in time for the meet. That left about 10 weeks, seemingly a tight scrape for the painter. I conferred with him, and he assured me that it would be ready at least a week ahead of the date. Promises, promises, promises.

Within the following week, our proud Lady presented the appearance of a sunken hulk at the bottom of the sea, including barnacles. She had been raised on jacks all around, the wheels were off, fenders and doors had been dismantled, windshield and all chrome fittings stripped. She was a pitiable sight. She looked even more horrible a week later, as most of the paint had

1936 Auburn "852" Boattail Speedster with master and exhausted pit crew

1956 Bentley, 1936 Auburn, and 1927 Rolls Royce

been stripped off in big blotches, and the bare patches of metal exposed the years of hairline cracks and ripples, which we had all anticipated. It was all par for the course, and only stamina and a quixotic imagination were needed to proceed with utter confidence.

Three weeks later, very little more had been accomplished, and we began to feel that first familiar clutch of anxiety. Other work had come into the shop in normal routine, this too was to be expected. Both Bobbie and I began our daily regimen of gentle prodding, coaxing, and reminding the kindly little gentleman that only five weeks remained until showtime.

He remained calm and conciliatory. "Please don't worry!" he counseled, all was under control. He was so ultra-courteous, agreeable, and cooperative (a welcome change) that it was virtually impossible to be severely critical. He certainly was doing a great job of it so far, and we calmed ourselves with this bromide.

Soon afterward he proved to be as good as his word; the body work and base preparation were completed. The Rolls now stood camouflaged under a crazy quilt of red and gray sealer and primer. Then the first three coats of black lacquer were applied, followed by the fawn-colored sections. Sanding and smoothing continued, and the next three coats of paint applied, and so on. This went on for about three weeks, and the compounding was next. The result was fabulous. We congratulated ourselves on a fine professional selection.

It was now a bit more than two weeks to deadline, and we began to breathe easier. The engine and accessory parts were de-gunked, sanded, primed, and resprayed with high temperature black enamel. Some fresh wiring was put in at this time, in critical areas, again for cosmetic purposes only. The wheels were next, but we ran into a small problem during a two-day rainspell. Lacquer needs clear weather to dry properly (how well we knew!) and we watched the weather reports impatiently. Luck was with us, it turned dry right to the end of the job. The wheels were marvelous.

Chrome replacement was next on the list. The trunk rack was reassem-'bled, and the Rolls started to emerge magnificently, the two-tone colors perfectly complementing each other, and reflecting that deep down lacquer gloss so vital to high point results. All that remained was final waxing, and completion of enameling of the chassis, which had been sandblasted to the base iron. We felt absolutely secure at that stage. Our plans were to bring her home the Wednesday before the show to do our own minute, fine detailing.

On Monday Bobbie phoned me at the office, wailing. Our painter had sprained his ankle on Sunday and was confined to bed for an indefinite period. I almost went into a spin—that old black magic was at work again! I settled down and considered the possibilities. The assistant in the shop was mainly a sander-and-polisher. I had never remembered seeing him handle the spray guns or do any of the master work. True, the undercarriage was not the most critical job. He could undoubtedly complete the priming—but who would do the final enamel shooting? On Tuesday morning at 8:00 A.M., wearing old pants and working clothes, Bobbie and I arrived at the paint shop. A three-way phone conference with the owner, mostly a babble of instructions and admonitions, launched us on the final job. I stayed an hour, spread-eagled on the floor under the Rolls, inspecting, scraping out rust in crevices, and talking things over with the other man. I then took off for my plant, leaving Bobbie in charge of the project until I could return at 5:00 P.M. Several phone calls during the day proved her capability again—things were proceeding nicely, she said, not to worry! Rushing back later, I found her on a rolling dolly, covered with powdery rust flakes, chippings, dried grease, and the road grime of decades. So much for the sandblasting theory— it never gets up into the entrails! The Rolls was now ready for final under-spray.

As a precaution, the entire completed body of the car was then wrapped completely in huge plastic drop cloths taped to the hubs (over blankets), so we weren't worried about any injury to the finished exterior. It was agreed that the spray would go on Wednesday morning, and the shop assistant was confident of his ability to lay on a smooth coating of the fast drying weatherproof chassis enamel.

Philosophically, that evening, we concluded that we might have some point loss in bottom judging for Kings Bay because of the incident, but what could we do?

On Wednesday morning, when we arrived, the assistant was already under the car, compressor rattling, shooting the enamel. One quick glance confirmed his inexperience. The paint was flowing on unevenly, heavy in some spots, lumpy on the axles. But it was too late to fuss about it. There was our grievous chapter ending on this paint job, and the Rolls would have to wait for the next big show to have her undersides partially refinished again.

That evening, a day later than intended, we remounted the ornery windshield and other chrome items. At mignight, disappointed and weary, finger-sore and aching in all bones, we drove our Rolls home, maligning the occult

After the restoration, the Rolls is now black-and-fawn and has new leather, chrome, and canvas.

curse of the paint shops. Only one fact gave us solace. It was Wednesday, and we still had two days to play with the points of finesse.

The Kings Bay show was a great success, *we* were not. With vital points lost underneath we scored Third Place in the meet. The two better cars in our class were really superb, so we didn't feel too badly after all. It would have been almost impossible to beat them anyway, and with a fresh car just out of the works, there are always areas of improvement that slip by in the final panic. We now had plenty of time to prepare for the big official autumn shows, and we were therefore gratified with the praise and comments from the club members, the public viewers, and even the judges, who unanimously

The massive old "iron head" Rolls Royce engine, restored, showing dual ignition and twelve spark plugs.

Trunk detail of the Rolls, showing sharp definition of the two-tone paint job.

felt that we had performed miracles in so short a time. Besides, I was so busy taking part in the management of the meet, preparing the trophy displays, and judging "late classics" that I barely had time to worry about it.

Another phase in the hobby, one that inevitably comes along from time-to-time, had developed during that period. We had gotten into negotiations with a Northern collector for the possible sale of the Lagonda. Over the years this faithful front-runner had won almost every major award possible in Florida, and most of the taste-pleasure had dissipated, like a bottle emptied of fine wine. We also had the firm belief that it's not fair to new-

Interior view of the Rolls cockpit: all the wood surfaces are refinished, the instruments gleaming. Note rear passenger windscreen. The rearview mirror is temporary.

comer cars for the same old winners to appear endlessly in competition. Unfortunately, not all our cohorts take this posture, as we were to learn again to our dismay with the Rolls the following year. I personally hope and expect that some uniform code of honor will be applied to this situation in the near future.

The negotiations for the sale of the Lagonda were concluded successfully. After years of pleasure and pride of ownership, we again suffered the pangs of regret and sentiment as we loaded the white giant onto the professional trailer-rig that had been sent down for the transfer to the new owner in New York. Goodbye dear old friend, we sighed, as the trailer wound up around the curves at the top of our street.

Another important and rich phase of our life with cars had ended.

POSTSCRIPTS BY MY WIFE

My determined mate put the King's Bay show together so quickly it didn't have a chance to get on all the club calendars around the state, and many car enthusiasts were unable to make it. Then too most of the Florida winter residents had returned North by the end of May, and that lost quite a few. Therefore, a local club edict was put out for members to bring as many cars as possible to make a good showing. We decided that we'd take the BMW as well as the Rolls, since we'd completed quite a bit of work on the little German beauty and she was certainly ready for competition.

On show morning Alan and the boys left early in the Rolls; he had some officiating to do and was in a hurry. I was to follow afterwards with the BMW. There was no problem there that I could foresee since I drove her almost every day. So I dressed leisurely and had another cup of coffee. No picnic today, there was marvelous food at the club, and we had invited friends for lunch. I stretched and yawned with pleasure.

Too soon! How come I always select white, pink, or pastel clothes for car shows? Dressed in yellow shantung, I slid smoothly into the snappy black and cream convertible, ready for a lovely day at the club. I turned the key, waited for her fuel pump to quit ticking, and depressed the pedal to get the fuel up into the carbs. That usually got it ready to roar—if the starter was in the mood. She gave one feeble grind, then I heard a pang and a ping, then a loud swat, and then silence. Sighing and groaning, I jumped out, raised her bonnet, and feverishly tried to find the trouble. Der Fleidermaus (my name for this gal) had sung her laughing song for me. The steel gas pedal cable had chosen this moment to snap in two, causing the linkage to the throttle to come apart, and there dangled the pieces like a collapsed marionette.

I tried my best, but it was too much for me, complicated by the lateness of the hour. With a brush-away of dust on my slacks, and a wipe of goo off my hands, I drove to the show in our Detroit Iron. Too bad. The BMW competition that day was puny; she'd have taken a First Place for sure! Did you happen to notice? I make no comments about the Rolls at the paint shop. Too much is too much.

11

A Brace of Racers

 Among the active exchange of letters that crossed the Atlantic in 1968 was a singularly exciting one from a supposedly reputable vintage car dealer in the middle-country of England. What had so tittilated my collector's "touch nerve" was a set of pictures of a big 1936 convertible 8-liter Hispano-Suiza, one of the world's five greatest marques (the others, in my opinion: Duesenberg, Rolls Royce, Bugatti, Isotta-Fraschini). The statements and allegations made in the letter were no less than hair-raising, with claims that the "Hisso" was, and I quote accurately, "undoubtedly a 100-point gem, the best example of its kind in the world," etc. Knowing this to be a virtual impossibility from tortured experience, we wrote back incredulously, asking for complete details about this photogenic phenomenon, which from the pictures submitted seemed to bear out the writer's gyrations. But one must never judge by that, at 10-foot camera range, though his answer stoutly confirmed his original statements, with all details covered in depth. It certainly appeared legitimate—there was no reason to believe otherwise. Plans were made to fly to London as part of the summer vacation-business trip to Europe.

We could hardly contain ourselves as the plane landed at Heathrow Airport. As anyone knows who has taken the night flights to London, you arrive about 7:30 A.M. disheveled, messy, red-eyed, and aching for your hotel, a bath, and a day to sleep it off. Not so on this pilgrimage. We couldn't wait to see the Hisso.

Half-asleep, we bulled our bags through customs, rented a car at the airport terminal, and started northward at once. It was a lovely, warm En-

This is the picture of the alleged "100 point" Hispano-Suiza that lured us to England.

glish morning, but in groggily adjusting to driving on the "wrong" side of the road, the 60-mile trip was pure hell. We got lost a few times, had to retrace our route about 5 miles, and stopped twice for coffee (try finding coffee at English pubs in the early morning!). We hung on resolutely, the shimmering image of the Heavenly Hisso dancing before our drooping eyelids. Finally we spotted our destination! I pulled in eagerly, crossing a busy intersection, on the *wrong* side of the road, unaware of the traffic problem I might have caused. No one was in the courtyard, but the big garage door was open. Both of us burst out of the car, barged right in, and got our first distant glance of the Hispano-Suiza. I hurried over to it at a dog trot and stopped short, dumfounded at what confronted me. Bobbie arrived a second later, huffing, expectant. What met our disbelieving glare was a panorama of rust spots, peeling paint, pitted chrome, worn tires, cracked leather, and shabby canvas. My hackles rose (and I really have handsome hackles).

Bobbie glowed with a slow burn in the cheekbones. She looked at me helplessly, also aghast at the nefarious information that had been sent to us in the mails. I snapped angrily, "How the devil is this possible? What's the point?" We were almost incoherent with anger. Enter from stage left, a tall, thin man. Still sputtering, I announced who we were.

"Oh, yes, we are expecting you," he beamed. "How do you like this magnificent car?" he asked proudly.

Overcome by disgust, disappointment, and exhaustion, I growled, "You gotta' be kidding! Is this wreck what you call a 100-point gem?"

He bristled instantly at the razor edge in my voice. "What do you mean by that?" he demanded somewhat resentfully.

I didn't really know where to begin, and exploded again. "What a damned nerve you have inviting people to fly 4,000 miles to see this 60-point reminder of past glory! No, I take that back—it wouldn't score 50 points in the States. $15,000! You mean $1,500?" With that final lunge, I turned on my heel, Bobbie following, indignant to the roots at this blatant and contemptible breach of business ethics.

He followed us to the door, waving both arms excitedly. "Wait a minute, wait a minute," he pleaded.

Bobbie and I looked at each other, our signal flags flapping in the gale. "Let's get our *derrieres* out of this gyp joint," she said wearily. "What's the point of waiting for another con man to argue with!" Of course she was right. We strode out of the door, hopped back in the rental and headed back to London, with sound and fury almost all the way.

The following day, Sunday, we flushed the entire ludicrous episode from our minds, and prepared to enjoy the day in the country, following up an advertisement we had seen in *Motor Sport* magazine, the general equivalent of our *Road and Track* in the U.S. The announcement had invited all comers to attend the Annual Rolls Royce and Bentley Meet in Surrey, south of London. Almost recovered from the trip (and the Hisso), we drove down with high spirits and happy vacation thoughts.

Surrey. This is one of the Country Squire, super-charming, meadowland areas of England, with soft, hazy, rolling hills, green as can be in summertime and chirping with cicadas in the hot morning. Dotted with graceful old manor houses and expansive wooded estates; it's pure unadulterated England in an amber antique bottle. We felt great, anticipatory, glad to be alive. And we were on our way to a real Rolls-Bentley show. Too much, old boyo! So we wandered off the main road to look around—our first day, tourists'-view still unclouded. Naturally, we got lost. Driving on, we stopped at a country inn to inquire, after returning to the same dead-end country lane three times in a row.

The inn was a piece from a Delius tone-poem, and we momentarily became so enchanted we almost forgot about the car show. I hit my head on the low lintel doorway on the way in, and almost repeated the act with the huge hanging lantern on the way out. In between I had a good view of the cavernous stone fireplace, slanting, polished, red brick floors, oak-beamed ceilings, and the eighteenth-century, country-dressed serving maids. This was no idle put-together, I decided.

"We've got to come back here for lunch," I told Bobbie in the car, and headed back to the main road with my new instructions. We found that we were only a couple of miles from the show grounds, and soon came upon a crenellated yellow brick manor house, tucked deep in the shadows of the trees, at the end of another narrow country lane. This was it. "Unreal," I thought, all the right images usually served up to the American tourist, though well off the beaten track.

We drove through the great lion-perched stone gates, and swung into a cobblestoned courtyard, facing what appeared to be a line of stables at the rear of the main house. Several Rolls and Bentleys were parked about, but we could see this was not the main show area. We soon found the assembly of cars by walking along a flower-lined garden path out to a broad grassy meadow nearby. Strung out row after row into the distance was the prettiest array of fine automobiles we had ever seen in one place, at one time. Every imaginable Rolls and Bentley model, type, color, and vintage, covered the landscape, from the Edwardian period through veteran, classic, and contemporary custom models. Our urge was to run in every direction at once, but we restrained ourselves and started an orderly passage down the first aisle.

I was wearing a black blazer that day, with the bright AACA patch on the breast pocket. As we passed among the cars, our British hosts glanced at this badge with curiosity and interest. One chap waved and called out, "Welcome Yanks!" and we felt grateful for their warmth and friendliness. I felt a clap on my shoulder, and turned around quickly, surprised to see a handsome, tanned stranger smiling at me, wearing a patch of the Classic Car Club of America.

We both yelled simultaneously, "What are you doing here?" like long-lost brothers and struck up an immediate friendship. Then Bobbie was introduced.

"Come look at my 1935 Bentley Sedanca-Coupe," he invited. I was much impressed—here was an American showing his car in England! He led us down the grassy slope to where his Bentley was on display, a thoroughbred classic, painted that singularly handsome British Racing Green, trimmed inside with saddle-colored hide. In answer to my query about the car being shown here, he explained that he had bought it in London the previous winter, and left it for restoration to be ready for this show. Surreptitiously, casting a critical but judicious eye over the car, I noticed quite a few faults in paint and chrome. He must have caught the slight hesitation in my stance. "It's really not up to our crazy U.S. standards, is it?" he asked disarmingly.

I disliked being put on the rack so ingenuously by another American collector, but an honest question deserves an honest answer, particularly between compatriots. Before I could frame a tactful reply, he coaxed me some more. "Come on now, let's have an expert's opinion," he said. This challenge was based on the information we had already exchanged about our years of experience in restoration and our successes in the show world. Okay, I thought, here goes.

Starting kindly as an opener, I pointed out the flaws over which he had already, no doubt, shed his own tears. We went around the car together, checking off deficiencies at an alarming rate. He knew his car, I could see that, and it worried him plenty.

I backed off, embarrassed. "There's no doubt you'll win First Place here," I predicted.

"Yeah," he said wryly, "but the competition is pretty puny!" We both laughed at this truism. He knew how the British concentrated on mechanics, too.

I learned in the next moment that he had laid a little harmless trap for me. He chuckled, "I've already raised hell with the restorer. The car is going back to him for a major rework right after the show!" Then came the punch line. "How about your support if I should need it?" Canny chap. It was all the same to me—he certainly was justified in being dissatisfied with the final result on the great car, and I agreed.

Our new friend hit it off with Bobbie right off the bat. He had a swinging Continental savvy that she liked in a man, and I guessed shrewdly that he liked her sporty looks. She looked particularly great that day, hair and silk scarf blowing in the breeze, impish as always, flirtatious and gay. He had good taste in women! Leaving them to their joshing and animated conversation, I wandered around the show, marveling as always at the perfection of British engine restoration for daily use, and, conversely, at their indifference to sharp appearance physically. Nice is nice, they say, so why get nervous about paint? Seems to me sometimes they may be right. It pleased me however to note that there was not one Rolls Royce rear windscreen touring phaeton in the bunch. They're rare even in England, as I well knew.

My wife and the Bentley owner were still engrossed in car talk when I strolled back. It was lunch time by then, and I invited him to join us at the picturesque inn down the road. He accepted, but first steered us back to the main house.

"Let's have a beer in the Tower Pub," he suggested. He certainly knew his way around the place. We found out later that he was a recognized authority among the British collectors; many of them had been friends of his for many years as he had enlarged his collection.

The Tower Pub, reached by ascending a narrow, spiral staircase, was a popular feature of this manor house compound that was part private home, part commercial club. It was the headquarters of the Rolls Royce-Bentley organizations in England. We stepped into the heavy-beamed, stuccoed-walled, mullioned-windowed, low ceilinged room amid a din and clamor reminiscent of the legendary Whiffenpoofs. It was protypically an English Pub—everyone present was engaged in earnest, often noisy argument, and laughter abounded. Groups of car collectors were clustered at tables, others crowded over the tiny bar—the room was jammed. This was the clubby British bit we hear so much about that is never really successfully emulated in the States. Our friend elbowed and fought his way over to the bar, with us in tow. Without asking, he ordered three gin gimlets, plunked Bobbie down on a bar stool, and then introduced us to the club director, who was also, incidentally, the bartender. Like any good American fund-raiser, he immediately tried to sell us a membership. We were very flattered to accept the membership form, but it amused us just the same.

We had a good opportunity during the slowly-served luncheon at the old inn to learn more about our new friend. His collection in New York included a very rare Rolls Royce Henley Roadster, reputedly one of three in existence at the time, an equally rare 1931 Cadillac V-16 touring phaeton, several other fine European cars, and a modern Rolls sports saloon. With dessert, he told us about his special brand-new Rolls Royce convertible that he'd just had custom built. It was to be delivered to him the following week, and then he and his wife were driving it to Cannes. The way he described this car overwhelmed my peach melba, which was mouth-watering enough by itself. This convertible, he told us, had been specially constructed on a seven-passenger chassis to afford more space in the rear, a la the early Maharajah jobs. It was lacquered in Brazilian coffee nut brown, to be precise, with tobacco-brown leather, and deep-pile plush carpeting especially woven for the car with a red-and-yellow fleur-de-lis pattern.

I began to wonder about all this opulence. He surprised me again by intuitively insisting that we go see the car in the Conduit Street showroom of the Rolls Royce Company in London, where it would be on display for a day or two prior to its final servicing for the trip to the Riviera. I certainly resolved to do this! We parted with friendly promises to see each other in Cannes in about two weeks. On Monday, before starting my business appointments, we strolled over to Conduit Street, half in doubt about the whole story. We inquired of the salesman who greeted us at the massive door, about the special convertible. We mentioned our friend's name, and

The 1934 Aston-Martin outside the garage of Vintage Autos, Ltd., Brooks Mews, London, with Jack Bond and the author.

were told that it had just been removed from the premises and had gone to the service depot. Too bad, he said politely, but could he show us some other new Rolls, perhaps? We got out of there fast—this was no $10 club membership he was talking about!

The next morning started out more in our usual style. We initiated our car ritual in London on every visit by making Jack Bond the first Port of Call. This was a tradition we enjoyed enormously, but it usually whetted our appetites for more cars, which was a tradition we did not always enjoy financially. As usual, Jack had some great cars. Nose-by-nose in front of the garage nested a pair of charming small classics; on the left was a beautifully balanced 1934 Aston-Martin four-seater tourer, indigo blue, with glittering, exposed chrome flexible exhaust tubes and muffler. Exquisite! On the right, beside the Aston, was a 1932 MG-K Magnette four-seater tourer, about the same size, with cream-colored body, red gull-wing fenders, and red leather interior. This car needed quite a lot of cosmetic restoration, but together the

The 1932 MG-K "Magnette" out in the mews. It has a surprising amount of space for two big men!

pair were almost irresistible. Jack dropped the special-price-for-two bomb again. But we resisted—it was the Aston we really wanted.

Behind the two small cars, gleaming in the dim rear area of the small garage, we noticed the majestic Rolls Royce Dual-Cowl Phaeton Jack had written about earlier in the year. It was a 1926 Ghost, impeccably lacquered in pearl gray, with a soft, black, glove leather interior. The restoration was as absolutely flawless as Jack had said it would be. He knew the score about American judging standards! We marveled at the mahogany side rails and running boards, brand new and dazzling under the clear lacquer coatings. Even the toolbox and top braces were almost like glass-finished mahogany. It really got you right here, in the belly. I had written Jack earlier that we had already found and restored our Rolls that same year, and we lamely reminded him of that fact, as our willpower drained away.

"What's wrong with having two of them?" he asked.

"I knew you'd ask that question, you miserable sadist," I groaned.

Though we hated to admit it—we had to swallow a good portion of pride—this Rolls was one of the greatest of its type in the world. But it had come too late. We stayed awhile, inspecting and fingering it longingly, though I sternly told myself it was obviously out of the question. Jack veered off standard course. He's always one you can count on for a new idea.

"Why not think of it as an investment? When you get it home you can decide which of the two you like better, and then sell one off at a nice profit."

Nothing doing! We resolutely turned back to the brace of small cars; our second response was the same as the first. We were hooked there, it seemed. One for Bobbie, one for me! Jack smelled the sale of the pair and dropped his price a bit further, with no prompting from me at all. That's when he really tried to get us with a better idea.

"How about a really *special* deal on the three cars?" he said slyly.

I grabbed a nearby tire iron off the floor and lifted it menacingly. "How would you like a special deal on a plain pine coffin?" I threatened.

"Okay, okay. I guess I got carried away with my desire to see you really happy, Alan," he said grandly. I remembered that he had been a movie actor in his early days.

"You ham!" I kidded. "Go sell your wares to the Dream Merchants."

He laughed. "Sleep on it," he said politely.

We got out of there in a hurry, the same old dragon spewing love-smoke in our eyes; we still had to struggle to smother those fires.

The rest of the week, in and around other appointments, we made our regular London rounds to the group of dealers who offered the type of classics we most enjoyed. They liked our dollars, so it was a fair joust. Our visit to Dale's again served up a mouth-watering feast. There was an Adonic black 1935 Bentley 3-position drophead coupe, a pair of Rolls open-front Sedanca de Villes, a Ghost tourer of the mid-twenties, and an assortment of Bentleys. The one that started my feeling of rapture was a 1955 Special One-Off fastback James Young Rolls Royce. I still wanted a great classic-styled car for daily use—the sweet, darty BMW had unhappily not ever filled that bill. This Rolls looked like the answer, with its unique swept-back body configuration separating the black over maroon lacquer. It was in superior condition, needing only a little leather renovation, and the price was incredibly low for the desirable James Young nameplate.

Bobbie caught the scent. Without even waiting for my first reactions, she hopped into the driver's seat and started pushing the pedals, maneuvering the big wheel, and annoyingly exaggerating the mass of the car.

"I could never drive this lorry," she announced with flat finality. "It's a clunker from way back," she said, in her own inimitable way when she wants to hold me down. "And, furthermore, you need the legs of a Decathlon Champion to release the clutch!"

I shot her a wrathful, dirty look, and continued my inspection without any further acknowledgment of her little-girl bad behavior. I knew how to fix her wagon, as she had tried to fix mine.

Sneaking up on her from the rear, I dug her in the ribs, and whispered fiercely, "I'm going to smash your rolling dolly when we get home, and then you'll have to lie on the greasy floors!"

But no logic reached her ears about the J. Young beauty. I tried the Jack Bond treatment: this unique body was a great investment; it could only increase in value; think of the fun we'd have driving up to restaurants and hotels, etc. No logic touched her.

"You ham!" she said cunningly, "Go sell your wares to the Dream Merchants."

What're you gonna' do with a memory like that?

But I knew the *real* reason. Those two little racer-tourers were swimming around in her bloodstream, and she wasn't going to let me take pills for *my* malady. Considering that our marital join-up has always been a pretty fair partnership, she has to be allowed to think she's a formidable opponent once in awhile, especially when she really decides to be. As a good politician, however, she conceded that it would merit some further discussion. On the other hand, I wasn't exactly opposed to the pair of glossy rabbits at Jack Bond's.

A couple of days later we settled the matter without argument—we bought the racers from Jack, and left for the French Riviera. To this day, I still deeply regret walking out on the glorious swept-side Rolls, and with the passing of time Bobbie has contritely admitted more than once, "It may have been a mistake."

POSTSCRIPTS BY MY WIFE

Smash my rolling dolly indeed. I don't really think so!

Since I had learned (when we painted the Lagonda) how great they were for working under the cars, I kept asking Alan to get me one for the garage. Enough of this foolishness of lying on my back on the hard, cold, concrete floor, squirming this way and that to avoid the oil drippings. Enough of lying on canvas mats and leftover corrugated cardboard sheets! He kept promising, and I wondered if he'd forgotten. That's not like him, though, so I kept hoping.

When Mother's Day rolled around that year, he handed me a large, flat box tied with a big red bow on it. Hello Dolly! How thrilling. What more could a Mother ask?

I wonder if I'll ever live down that James Young Rolls at Dale's. I pointedly remember a conversation I had with an English cinema director who was also there shopping for a "nothing" Rolls for a big movie scene, while Alan was making the scene with the big maroon baboon. Plot: seems a kooky young society girl drives her husband's classic Rolls into their swimming pool in a fit of pique. She is obviously unhappy in the marriage, and next she has a love affair on the side with her husband's best friend. The errant lovers soon come to realize the impossibility of their ill-starred romance (what with the extra guilt tonnage and so on) so they agree to commit suicide together by driving off a cliff. But get this—they go over the edge side-by-side in two cars while holding hands! How? She's in a right-hand drive British sports car, and he's in a left-hand drive Italian jobbie. What a dreadful waste of cars (and what else?) in that movie. Two things: I don't want a Rolls in our pool. Also, romantics that we are, I guess the story helped in deciding to buy the brace of racers.

12

A Wet Little Escapade

 Both cars arrived at the Miami docks in mid-September, 1968, scrupulously wrapped, taped, and protected by our dependable man in London. Even the stevedores, who see a variety of automobiles arriving from European ports, evidenced great excitement as we rolled them out of the shed onto the wharf. Water was run into the radiators, oil checked, gas put into the tanks. The sweet, throaty sound of both highly-tuned engines sang out at the first try of the starter buttons. What a pretty pair of mantlepiece bric-a-brac they would make.

We had decided to drive them home in tandem, tops down. Bobbie would take the simpler gear-shift Aston-Martin, and I would drive the Magnette with its tricky pre-selector Wilson gear box. Both cars had ample seat and leg space for me, unusual in these small racing type bodies. Would we have bought them otherwise? Motors were warmed, we revved up, and started for home happily waving to each other as we headed up the causeway ramp leading across the bay. We were stopped by a traffic light at the foot of the ramp, on a rather steep incline. With a slow engine roll and a cough, the MG stalled on the slope.

Honking the horn at Bobbie in front of me, I signaled that I would roll back to the flat grass area beside the road. But the the MG refused to start up again, and in minutes, the battery went dead. It had obviously pooped out during the month long sea voyage, and the balky devil had had it, and so had I. We hailed a passing truck, explained our predicament, and obtained a $2 rope-tow back to the docks. We left her in a safe, temporary parking slot in the workshed, which was arranged by the friendly dock boss for another

$5 bite. With his sympathetic clucking following behind us, we departed together in the Aston-Martin.

During this extended and vexing operation, the sky had turned quite black—it was thunderstorm season in Miami. We decided to make a run for it anyway, and bolted up to the causeway, glancing up uneasily at the sky. I was tempted to put the top up, but before I could make up my mind to do so the skies opened up with a big bang and lots of brilliant lightning, so we had no choice but to keep going until we got to the other side of the bay. Down came the pelting waterfall, soaking us in the open tourer. We raced across the causeway to the other side and slammed into a Sunoco station, blowing the horn and gesturing wildly for the attendants to open the garage doors. They looked out at us through the streaming rain, and shrugged callously. Who was kinky enough to go out in this deluge? Groaning with frustration, we jumped out of the car and fought to raise the canvas top in the wind and slashing downpour and finally got it latched to the posts. Then we got back in the car, concerned for the panel instruments, and satisfied ourselves that no water had gotten behind them. We realized that we were drenched to the skin, and our shoes were squelching little bursts of rainwater over the soaked carpets.

"What the heck are we sitting here for?" I asked in astonishment. With that gentle point of logic, we stepped out of the car and leisurely proceeded to the station office where Bobbie sweetly thanked the gentlemen inside for their gallantry, draining streams of water spitefully over their scrubbed tile floor. They were too abashed to make any comment.

She went into the ladies' room to make repairs. I stripped off my jacket, shirt, undershirt, shoes, and socks—everything but my pants, and wiped dry with paper towels which were silently handed to me. One of the men had the decency, at the sight of all the ruin, to offer the loan of a nylon zipper jacket, courtesy of Sunoco, emblem and all. I promised to return it the next day. Then Bobbie came out, a big roll of sodden clothes clutched in her arms. She had found a large, dry silk scarf in her handbag, and had wrapped it about her upper torso like a Dorothy Lamour sarong. I looked at her appreciatively, as I'm sure did the others.

"Don't get fresh!" she said archly, and the next thing you knew we were hiccupping with laughter. I stopped wheezing long enough to say, "If we had bought the James Young Rolls, we could have shut the *windows!*" And this threw us into a further tizzy. So you see, in that small way, I had my revenge.

POSTSCRIPTS BY MY WIFE

That was some ride! When I started to drive the Aston (it was me!) I knew she was going to be a tricky little bird. Her gas pedal was between the clutch and the brake pedal, the gear shift was on the left in the middle of the car, and the emergency brake on the right, against the side wall. The Lagonda had been the same, so I'd already learned the game of tap-your-head and rub-your-belly with a fair amount of coordination.

That's all tricky enough, you'll agree, but in a smashing rainstorm it's quite a special event, especially when the windshield wiper suddenly jams in its tiny arc. So I had to drive with my head hanging out over the right side of the car, grabbing a look down every chance I could get to be sure I was on the right pedal. The rain was streaming down my face and I could have used a face wiper myself. But there was no place to pull over, so we made our mad dash for the gas station across the bay.

When the rain let up we finally headed for home, speedboating our way through some huge puddles. I said, jokingly, while pulling at my makeshift halter, that all we needed was a big truck to swish by, and with that invitation, one obliged—a large van coming in the other direction plowed a tidal wave right into our laps. It was a good thing I was on the right side driving. Alan got the worst of that deluge.

But I was really happy. My Brace of Racers had arrived, and I had all sorts of rosy ideas about what fun it would be for me to have some cute small cars to play with. But I learned ruefully in the not too distant future that large, medium, or small they're all plagued with the same outlandish miseries. When will I learn to be a mousy little wife with no bright ideas of her own?

13

A Slight Switch in Taste

After the Lagonda was sold, we had moved the fat Mercedes-Benz into the garage with the Rolls. With the arrival of the two cars from Britain, we moved the Mercedes into the enclosed carport. That meant shifting the BMW to the other side of the house, under a forest green 20' x 10' vinyl canopy tent recently installed for that purpose. The Jaguar had been sold to a young lawyer in order to make space for the MG-K under a giant Schefflera tree (or Queensland Umbrella) which afforded adequate shelter for this diamond in the rough. The Aston-Martin then got the position of honor next to the Rolls. What a strange contrast—the huge, ponderous, ocean liner and the sleek, racy, torpedo boat. Even with the canvas top up in place on the Aston, the total height of the pantherlike sports car only reached up to the door sills on the Rolls Royce.

With all the cars thus cozily located and well protected, we did an analysis of the line-up regarding comparative potentials, personal preferences, and work required for each car vis-à-vis the forthcoming Meets on the Fall-Winter schedule. It was decided that the Aston would be shown at the first opportunity, the AACA Pier 66 Concourse in Fort Lauderdale.

The Rolls was also registered for this show, and that meant some rush work on both, though no major jobs were slated for either; only some fine detailing, traditionally the owner's specialty. The Aston of course had first call, we knew precisely how little the Rolls required to seat her on the pinnacle of first place. In researching our ideas for the Aston, we had discovered that these cute leprechauns were sometimes painted the racing colors of a particular team. From photos of similar short-chassis A-M's delectably two-toned by painting the body and cycle wings in contrasting color, and the wheels a third color, we started our restoration program. We put the car into a big commercial paint shop, with a one-week promise of delivery. On pickup we were pleased with the sporty, baby blue fenders on the indigo blue body, and the bright red brake drums were a spicy background relief for the 19'' silver spoke wheels. Some minor chrome work was also completed at the same time.

Bobbie then put her masterful hand to the engine cosmetics. Obviously a woman's small hand, accustomed to eyelash makeup, was better than the hand of a man for this refined tight-space artistry, after, of course, a thorough degreasing of the engine compartment. The block was enameled in authentic red, cast aluminum panels and covers were gently rubbed with aluminum-pigmented surface refinisher, the radiator core and frame were resprayed black hi-gloss enamel, and her undersides were steam-cleaned, and painted chassis black. The latter job was the dirty part, and here the man's hand came into play. We stared dubiously at the chrome door hinges, showing thin and yellow in spots. Should we get involved in this pesty job? Removing door hinges is chancy—they rarely go back easily, and sometimes the doors don't fit right afterwards. We decided to pass it by, and do it for some future show, although we surmised that a consistent prize-winning, small, racy Lagonda would show up in the same judging class to torment us. This ineffable red beauty had been lovingly restored by her owner, literally from a "basket case," over a five-year period, and the car was truly deserving of her awards. We knew it was a gamble to take the shortcut with the Aston, but it was time to get on with the Rolls, which had been waiting patiently in the wings.

We spent about a week on the undercarriage of the R-R, repairing the inept paint work applied so hurriedly before her first showing. The engine and body were polished to luminous peak, and, unbelievably, *two whole weeks* before the show both cars were wrapped up and ready for the event, quite a singular experience in our exhibitor career.

To be altogether honest, we were not really completely ready, as we still suffered some of the same old Rolls engine overheating and sputtering, despite two more trips to the mechanical shop. But since this was not a point category, and we knew we would not solve the mystery without a major carburetor and vacuum tank overhaul, we murmured a small prayer and hoped she'd make the 75-mile round trip without serious mishap.

The doughty little Aston-Martin, Second Place winner at the Fort Lauderdale AACA Meet.

Pier 66 is a phenomenal complex sponsored by the Phillips Petroleum Company. It consists centrally of a multi-story circular resort hotel, with a slowly rotating, glass-enclosed cocktail lounge on the top floor. This over-looks the city and a magnificent yacht marina, said to be one of the finest in the world for layout, size, and boating facilities. Some of the greatest yachts in the country dock here for the winter season. Against this plush and exotic tropical background the Meet was held in the hotel parking lot, adjacent to the graceful yachts bobbing up and down in the constant breezes that swept the area.

The trip up to the show was a pleasure. Bobbie drove the doughty Aston, carrying her mother and our son Jonathan. Bennett rode with me in the silent Phantom—the Rolls was always his preference. Only an occasional sputter brought our hearts to our mouths, but she docilely controlled her indigestion, and we made it to the show with mutual car-owner pride and affection. As we rolled into position in the lineup, we dismally spotted the two cars that would beat us for first place in both classes, the red perky Lagonda in the Aston class, and the great National AACA and Grand Classic First Prize winner, the van-delivered short-chassis 1929 Packard Roadster, showing in the same class as the Rolls.

And that's the way it turned out—we went home from the banquet with two Second Place silver bowls, another evidence of the deficient and out-moded system that allows the same unbeatable cars to win over and over again in Junior competition, when they necessarily should be in Senior competition with each other! Many owners, as a result, become gun-shy out of discouragement, and stay away from certain meets that offer no Senior class separation. There is a halfhearted trend to make the Senior rule apply, but as yet this is not a uniform agreement in all the major clubs.

The disconsolate trip home in the Rolls deserves some wry comment. As though deeply affronted by her second secondary win, she struggled her way home, coughing and wheezing and jerking, like a tired old horse on a hot, dusty day. We understood, and forgave.

We did win a different First Prize that day, however, with Bobbie's flapper costume in the Women's Division. She won the award with a short, side-slitted, pale green, crystal beaded tube dress that we had found the summer before in a funny little antique shop in Portobello Road, London. The rest of her outfit consisted of a vintage silver-framed beaded bag which she swung saucily in circles from its long chain, while exaggeratedly chewing gum with loud snaps. A 12" long cigarette holder completed the attire, all of it enhanced by the swinging hip motions of that era. And this she knows how to do.

Life settled down again after this mixed event. One day early in 1969, while driving down LeJeune Road in Miami, a '39 Cadillac Fleetwood caught my eye in a gas station, the red and white "For Sale" sign prominently displayed in the rear window. Mildly curious, I stopped to look. A few feet away I then noticed a faded maroon '67 Lamborghini 400 GT 2+2. Inquiring of the attendant, I learned that it too was for sale. To my surprise in checking it over, I found that this rare car was apparently in perfect condition. Only the paint was faulty. The interior fawn colored leather was in almost new condition, the engine was immaculate. This was indeed a mystery. Why was this exquisite automobile here of all places, and for sale? I was advised to inquire across the street at the C.I.T. office, where I learned that it had been repossessed from the owner. The paint deterioration was explained as having resulted from exposure to sun, salt-spray, and wind at the owner's beach house. Here was a prize indeed. The next day, almost compulsively, I returned with a sports car mechanic, satisfied myself that it was in perfect condition, and made my bid. The deal was consummated rapidly, as the loan company recognized the difficulty of quickly disposing of this rare, extraordinary machine. This was now the third departure for me

Bobbie in the flapper costume found in Portobello Road in London.

from the vintage car boundaries, but certainly the "Lamb" was a vintage car in its own right, as were the previous Jaguar and the big, blond Mercedes-Benz.

Within a week, the Lamborghini was in the reliable commercial paint shop that worked over the Aston. We selected a very special irridescent emerald green lacquer, the perfect foil for the natural colored leather interior. It was a marvelous paint job, and was further offset by an inspired covering of the hardtop roof with a creamy tan, padded vinyl top, installed by our favorite upholsterer in South Miami. When a renowned, international artist friend of mine, Frank Kleinholz, saw it for the first time, he exclaimed, "It's pure poetic sculpture!"

We now had moved up to a total of eight cars; 6 antique classics, a Buick Riviera, and a newly acquired Buick Electra convertible. The party in the courtyard was getting bigger all the time. It was decided, therefore, to sell the BMW posthaste to take the load off our parking facilities, and this was accomplished easily in a few days, without too much sentiment, via an ad in the *Miami Herald*.

The Lamborghini became our major plaything. It was also instrumental in making a warm friendship with a local resident, George Shelley, a true sports car fan. One day while swooping down our street around the big curve, I

The sleek and sculptured profile of the 400 GT Lamborghini explains the passion and the pride.

almost came nose-to-nose with a brilliant red 400 GT Lamborghini heading uphill in the opposite direction. We both slammed on the brakes, and exchanged animated "hello's." It seems George had heard there was now another Lamb in the area, and had come looking for it. We signalled him to make a "U" turn, and he followed us back to our house. Then and there we had the first Lamborghini rally in the Miami area! The two, still-panting, exotic speed demons were placed side by side (George called them Kissin' Cousins) and a series of photos was snapped with great pleasure.

This was the beginning of my tangential sports car compulsion. Several months later I heard about a perfect Silver/red leather 1968 Ferrari 330 GTC, and the virulent fever of the great Italian sports cars caught me in its grip for the second time. I brought it home on my wife's birthday as medicine and cure for a mild case of bronchial pneumonia she was battling at the time. We were now back to the apparently inescapable number of 8! The almost new Ferrari, which had belonged to a former racing car driver, was in immaculate condition, and needed only a good waxing and some leather-softening treatment. With both great Italian cars to choose between, my problem of conspicuous consumption became as challenging as deciding what color of tie to wear in the morning. To tell the truth, I did feel too opulent with both, and when the maintenance and repair problems began, I learned why there were so few of them around. As great as these cars are known to be, they are also as sensitive and skittish as thoroughbred racehorses. One standard problem in semi-tropical climates is the pulsing engine heat-buildup. It doesn't take very long for the needle to creep up past the "safe" line,

"First Annual Lamborghini Rallye." Note the difference in the roofline between the 400 GT 2+2 in foreground and the 400 GT 2-seater coupe behind it. The BMW got into the picture for classic relief.

while you're hung up in traffic in 90 degree weather. This in turn begets other difficulties such as plug and valve fouling and ignition burnout. It's routinely necessary to roar up the expressways heading nowhere in particular, and blow out the carbon, watching in the rear view mirror for a State Trooper. Even though only a minute may be required to pop the cork, try to explain 120 mph for half a mile to the guardians of our highways. In Europe there are no speed limits—so it's a lot easier to stay on top of this absolute requirement.

The subjective difference between the Lamb and the Ferrari, driving them alternately, was quite exhilarating. The Ferrari GTC, famous for its trans-axle, available only in this 330 GTC model, is a flyaway thundering machine, growling and roaring at the slightest acceleration of the gas pedal. It's a wild, "for kicks" car, and everyone admits that the fuss-and-feathers is deliberately built in for the owner's gratification. It also has the obvious danger in city traffic of engendering a heady bravura, an aural rapture that can spell trouble to the uninitiate driver and to adjacent automobiles! My eventual opinion, after more than a year of exercising prodigious self-control on the streets and expressways, was that this noisy roustabout is best suited to the Autostradas of Italy, and to their own citizens' fiery and debonair natures. What a perfect pair they make.

By contrast, the Lamborghini is a superb understatement of silken, silent power. Exhaust noises are refined and sophisticated—a smooth, harmonious tune, almost musical to the senses. Its thrust and getaway parallel that of the Ferrari without the frightening roar and fireworks; one feels a sense of security and pleasure that is a decided psychological safety factor. The utter perfection of this V-12, with its six Weber carburetors hissing whisper-soft, is one of the greatest feelings I have ever known behind the wheel of any motorcar. No wonder dual V-12 Lambs are installed in speed-record racing hull boats. Some have been wound up to over 200 miles per hour on the water.

After the eventual sale of this spiritually enriching automobile about a year later, I felt a strange regret and nostalgia, but conversely, memories of the GTC Ferrari are filled with delight and a sort of laughter-who-needs-it feeling. It was a great experimental period for me. Bobbie sort of watched with patient understanding and, I'm sure, much personal concern, until I had had my fill of both of these demanding objets d'heart, and finally disposed of them as a tribute to my life insurance policies.

During this aberrant interval, some guilt-making neglect for the classics was unavoidable. Certainly the time had come to get started on the 1932 MG-K Magnette, and we finally began the critical analysis process. The more we looked at the car, the more we agreed how nice it would be to restore this pretty classic for "regular daily use"—that chimera still beckoned us over the hill—and not bother to go all the way into the pressure cycle to prepare for show condition. There were quite a few snaky quarterdeck cracks in the aluminum where heliarc welding was needed, as well as numerous areas of engine, chrome, and cosmetic work. We agreed that a respectable restoration would suffice. (Sensibly, after the first few years of car competition is out of your system, you begin to dwell more and more on the pleasure side of the cars—how many years of grueling punishment can you take without being labelled a masochist?) This hobby *is supposed to be fun!* We certainly didn't covet any more trophies for their own sake. One joke among old-time collectors is that the smart thing to do at a certain point would be to trade in all your silverware for a good steak dinner. I can't say I agree with that casual approach, but it has its practical side.

The truth is that if it were not for show competition most of our wonderful automobiles might never be brought back to their original pristine beauty. To us, that's the real key, and the compelling purpose behind the art. Though we cuss and groan and complain all the way through a major restoration, we keep our eyes on that *raison d'être,* the ultimate and shimmering pie-in-the-sky: the beauty of the car and its near-perfection.

So that points up the contradiction in the whole matter. After you do restore to high-score peaks, you don't dare use the cars for pleasure while

The thundering Ferrari 330 GTC Transaxle devil has teeth bared, ready to devour fuel, children, cats, or anything else in the way.

you're on the competition merry-go-round. It's also worth noting that the special insurance policy available for the hobbyist clearly admonishes the policyholder that show cars are not to be employed for regular purposes. It specifically states that the moving coverage is in effect only for driving to shows, parades, exhibits, special events in connection with club outings, charity affairs, etc., etc. The protective policy is under threat of cancellation if an accident should occur under unauthorized circumstances, but as a reward for good behavior, the rates are amazingly low, and after the fourth car is covered in the policy, there is virtually no premium charge added for the next ten or fifty. What a boon for the collector with a warehouse full, and there are quite a few of them in the United States. It is also necessary, however, that the old machinery be kept moving to keep the juices flowing. To allow them to stagnate between shows is very dangerous. Our program for Saturdays is to do maintenance work and spruce-up around the collection, start them all up, and take them out in rotation, up and down the street for a workout. This keeps the clutch plates free of corrosion, blows out the carbon (in second gear, what a roar at 30 mph), and stirs up the gasoline so it doesn't jell into varnish at the bottom of the tank or the carburetor bowls. Neglect of this therapeutic procedure is sure to be punished by fretting and grouchiness in the old ladies, usually ending in balky recriminations. Like a ventriloquist and his weird fascination with his dummy, we've cagily learned not to hurt their feelings anymore. Run 'em weekly, change the oil regularly, clean the terminals of corrosion, check their valves and timing, and for God's sake, don't forget to adjust the clutch!

My modern classics, meantime, jealous no doubt of our ministrations to their elderly ancestors, would select the damndest times to "go down." This usually happened when we were all set to go out for the evening or a weekend. Seized by a sudden desire to drive the Lamborghini, I would ease my bulk into the snug seat, joyfully turn the key, and be greeted by a small burp and then a dead silence. "Too much attention to the old Rolls," I could almost hear accusingly in the echo of the starter. No dummy this siren. I occasionally considered dropping a lump of sugar down her radiator mouth. Sometimes I tried a loving pat on the fender, with a small pinch in the rear end, Italian Style, which worked wonders. So much for inanimate personalities. Please don't laugh.

The MG-K, still impersonally held at bay, had not yet found any loving nerve in our responses. To us at that time in 1969 and for some time to come, she was just a cute car with a rather distinguished history, but we did occasionally regret having brought her over, mainly because she did not fit into our pattern of "important" classics. One of the rare and redeeming features of this fine little car was the Wilson pre-selector gearbox. This type of box, often used in racing, can be jumpy, and requires periodic adjustment of the control bands. When operating smoothly it furnishes a swift and easy shifting method; you pre-select the gear desired on a vertical, numbered slot, move the gear lever, and press a button on the floor. It's really very pleasant —no clutch, no grind. However, poor band adjustments may result in a bolting getaway in first gear, with a resulting crawl in reverse. Otherwise, she is typical early MG, dependable, maneuverable, mechanically fine, and simple.

Our attentions to this perky rascal were never continuous, however. Each particular period of concentration took her several steps further, but always the demands of the others obscured hers. We did eventually complete the leather reupholstery, and the carpeting, and the minor heliarc welding. At that point, with body and paint to go plus chrome and a new canvas top, we covered her up again, and swung back to our other maintenance schedules. And there were plenty of these around.

POSTSCRIPTS BY MY WIFE
I really love that phrase, "Daily Use Classic." You know who ends up driving the old bags daily? You guessed it. While he drives the Ferrari!

Alan wouldn't think of driving them to the plant—they might get dirty, the sun would be on them all day, it might rain, there could be a hurricane. What else can he think of? So over the years, to assuage his conscience, I've driven many of these D.U.C.'s. One of these I really liked was the bright red 1957 Jaguar XK-140, a real sporty 2-seater roadster, and lots of fun—but only in warm, dry weather. I'd be driving along with 8 bags of groceries in the jump seat, a big boxer dog, and a small boy crammed up in front. I'd stop for a red light. Some kooky-looking character would pull up to me in a Triumph, MG, or Corvette and start flirting—until he saw the whole menagerie. Then he'd blast off without another glance, wondering what the heck all that was doing in a Jag. If I'd been so disposed I could have shown him a thing or two about dragging—kid, dog, soap-powder and all. Some nerve!

It was really fun when it rained—the bane of our existence in all vintage cars. In the Jag I had to scrootch down to get in under the little canvas top, and of course it had no windows, so I always carried an old raincoat to cover my left shoulder and lap. The rain always leaked through the windshield and ran down my legs. Boy, was that cold in January, even in Florida! But then you always looked so sporty and British Girl.

Those years I was doing charity work in a women's group that raised money for educating refugee children in Europe, and it became a running joke, "Hey, Bobbie, what are you driving today?" They came to know that I would usually have some hang-up when I drove one of the Classics. One day, dressed to the hilt for a fancy luncheon, I dashed out of the house and hopped into the Jag, my big picture hat catching on the top brace. That wasn't bad enough; this was the day the car decided to give up the ghost on the fuel pump, which had been gurgling up fair warnings for about a week. No worries, with all our cars around, who has problems? So I went over to the BMW, but Alan had been working on her starter and it was disassembled on the bench, so that was out, too. Then I tried the Mercedes, but since she had not been run much lately, her battery was dead. Alan had the Buick. There was only one other choice. I went to pick up my girlfriend in our prize-winning Lagonda!

Each one of our cars had a different shift system, and I could never remember which was which. The only way I could tell was to unsnap the leather coverlet around the gearshift lever, and peek. (Alan used to wonder how the covers got unsnapped all the time.) Anyway, I picked up Sylvia, and she rode all the way with one hand gripping each side of her seat, in sort of a downward prayer position. I don't know whether it was me or the car she didn't trust. Needless to say, we caused quite a sensation at the luncheon, as we were late and the girls were looking for us as we drove up in the gleaming white, regal Duke.

As they say, "If you've got to go, go in style!"

14

Fortune—and a Flight of Fancy

The vintage car shows came and went, and we decided to limit our attendance to a maximum of four a year, which pretty much kept those meets within 75 miles of home. More than a fair share of First Place trophies were added to our 1969 harvest. The Aston was beginning to make its mark, too. We headed into the new year with only one nagging problem, and it was getting more troublesome all the time.

With six to eight cars operating, our needs for mechanical and sustaining services had become rather ogerish. Every one of the cars was thoroughly understood, and each had its own distinctive set of pettish ailments. Since I am not really strong on the auto-mechanical side, many attempts had been made over the years to locate an all-around craftsman to service our cars, but in today's makeshift world the best that we ever found was the routine kind of patch-up work for Detroit Iron. So we lived on the bristly edge of frustration, finding partial solutions here and there, dealing with grumpy mechanics and controlling our patience with set jaws and a resigned attitude.

Luckily, fickle fortune had a big and pleasant surprise in store for us. In April, 1970, somewhat out of curiosity after a year or so with the Lamborghini and its insoluble electrical problems, the only weak spot in this lively member of our chorus line, I ran a "For Sale" ad in the local paper. The price tag was substantial, and I was pleased to receive four calls. One of them was from a young man who was destined to play a significant role in the mechanical implementation of our collection, and beyond that, in our personal lives.

Arthur Delman was the answer to a car collector's prayers. From a casual beginning when he came to see the Lamb, a tentative friendship soon developed. His extraordinary scope of knowledge and ability as he hovered in the background for the first several weeks at first amazed us. We realized that he had not come to buy the car, but only to have the pleasure of touching, looking, and dreaming about it. Then he dropped in one day with a complete manual on the MG-K and left it with us for review. He also offered to help with the MG-K and the rest of the cars, which he admitted floored him! We most willingly welcomed him, equally impressed by his versatile knowledge across the entire spectrum of fine machinery. He slowly began to tinker with certain surface problems that had been plaguing the cars. Whatever he touched eagerly responded at once, his sensitive hands and fine mind instinctively found simple solutions that had eluded many so-called experts. His heavy ten-year background with aircraft engines as a calibrating specialist at a large engine plant in Miami gave him an enormous "feel" for any trouble spot, and, added to that, he had grown up in a family of craftsmen and engineers.

We were soon able to discern definite improvements; our joy was boundless. A tacit understanding developed; he began phoning during the week, and then slipped naturally into regular Saturday visits. Nothing fazed him, he would just as soon tackle a problem on the Ferrari as on the ancient Rolls Royce. His first widely encompassing project was to flush out all the radiator systems, clear the rust out thoroughly, and then refill with a special miscible oil that he guaranteed would drop the temperature range of old and new alike at least 10 degrees. He was absolutely right—even the Ferrari ran cooler in traffic. In the meantime, one of the other interested callers on the Lamborghini ad became enamored of the gem-green teardrop beauty, and to our distress he arrived one day, with a fistful of $100 bills! What else was there to do? We reluctantly said goodbye to this elegant vintage masterpiece.

Our Saturdays with Arthur now had a definite purpose; the big approaching May AACA Meet at the Seaquarium in Miami was only a few weeks away. As the tempo and the extent of the projects increased, we invited him to bring his family along, and this too soon became a weekly ritual. Arthur was fascinated at becoming part of the show world, and keenly looked forward to his first show with our cars. We decided to exhibit the Rolls and the Aston again, some minimum improvements having been achieved by show time. Both cars were filled to the gunwales with the two families as we drove onto the grounds. We agonizingly discovered that the red Lagonda and the mighty, invincible Packard roadster were both on hand again, the same two cars that had espaliered our same two cars out of First Place at the Pier 66 show.

We suffered the same depressing defeat again, taking Second in both divisions against these near-100-point cars. It was then that we finally resolved that we would stay away in the future from such carelessly planned shows with no Senior classes. It was obvious that our own generous attitude with our erstwhile white Lagonda was not a universal one, and we felt that other car owners should follow this same precept. We could not comprehend the purpose of filling closets with repetitious trophies, while newer restored cars faced sudden death at the hands of these unbeatable winners. To be honest, I believe that most collectors feel as we do. It's damnable to meet the National champions head-on over and over again.

To add to our woes at this meet, one of the taillights on the Rolls got balky, and flickered during the judging. Arthur rapidly pulled the rim and found a burnt-out wire. With brilliant finesse he picked up a piece of chewing gum aluminum foil wrapper and created a perfect contact between the points, but it was too late—the judges had moved on. Furthermore, topping this emergency, one of the judges was our old friend from years before, who never (I think) forgot the tiny gouge I found on the leatherette roof of his fine Lincoln limousine, thereby losing the 1/2 point to the very Packard that was now giving *us* such a bad time at the local shows. Poetic justice? Without looking hard, he found a few rough spots on the undercarriage. With pencil flying, he recorded these demerits on the score sheet. Both of our cars took Second Place again.

It was not all bad, however. One funny little story deserves telling. In the milling throng that day was another of the sweet, omnipresent elderly ladies who ask the most disarming questions. After two or three cooing tours around the 1927 Rolls, she approached me. "Have you had this beautiful car since it was new? " she asked meekly.

I guess the gloomy mood I was in was part of the reason for my grumpy reply. "Yes, Madame, my father gave it to me for my seventh birthday." My little joke didn't register, and she walked away mulling over this leg-pulling, while I was left standing with a very, very guilty feeling.

More joy was yet to follow. On the way home, with the Delman family in the Rolls, we suddenly started overheating about a mile and a half from home. Chugging and gasping, she finally konked out in the 95 degree heat, as I barely rolled to a shady spot under a tree. I opened the bonnet in exasperation as Bobbie and Arthur in the Aston-Martin pulled in behind us. We sent Bobbie home in the Aston, and she shortly returned in the Riviera bringing tools, ice water, a bucket of sympathy, and a tow-rope. During this time Arthur had made several key evaluations: (1) the vertical manifold pipe, which heats up cherry red and is positioned between the fan and the carburetor system, was obviously forcing its extreme heat toward the carburetor, thereby causing a vaporizing of the gasoline; (2) the fan belt was pretty floppy; and (3) there was a new build-up of rust flakes in the radiator.

This overall analysis gave us some indication of what would need to be done. Wrapping the manifold in woven asbestos webbing would be one of the answers, he said, plus a new fan belt properly snugged up on the pulleys, and, lastly, another complete flush-out of the radiator, this time with a special heavy-duty cleaner, followed by a high proportion of coolant. To make absolutely sure we would be rid of this annoying problem forever, it was decided to pull the whole complex carburetor package and do a total overhaul. I agreed wholeheartedly with the entire diagnosis-and-treatment plan.

While we theorized under the trees, we bathed the carburetor in ice packs, ignoring the hoots and catcalls of passing motorists who inconsiderately yelled soothing and original suggestions like, "Get a horse!" After a series of adjustments and the careful trickling addition of ice water into the radiator, we were able to start her up and limp home, bucking and spitting. At least we were saved the ignominy of the tow rope through an area where more than one person would recognize the vaunted Rolls Royce.

Another important experience in the never-ending roller-coaster ride in the life of a vintage car collector happened that year. In the early spring, during a business trip to Chicago, I called to say hello to a well-known semi-professional car dealer, and to inquire idly about his current stock-in-trade. We do this routinely to keep in touch with the changing trends in prices and attitudes about antique and classic cars. He invited me over one evening to chat, as he too restocked his storehouse of information by talking to collectors from various parts of the country. He had three cars on hand, and I looked them over with polite interest. He always had his sights set on dozens of other cars around the nation, and was able to lay out before me a veritable feast of cars via photos, mostly in color. This is sport in itself While I had no intention whatsoever of buying another car at the moment, a door is always left slightly ajar for the rare or irresistible car. Our conversation inevitably came around to the big, fascinating subject. "What's doing these days in the Duesenberg market?" I asked rather absently, as a pretense.

"Same old story," he replied, "but only worse!"

We ranged over our common knowledge, mentally canvassing the few top dealers who always seemed to have one or two "Dueseys" on hand. Several private collectors were mentioned, and we agreed that the prices on these cars were skyrocketing out of sight.

Unexpectedly, he asked if I was really interested in a big open touring Duesenberg. I waved my hand in front of my face like a Japanese who has just stepped on your toes. "At today's prices, I'm really not jumping up and down with desire!" I answered wryly.

I was also thinking about the general let-down mood in business and financial circles in the Spring of 1970, and cash was a pretty scarce commodity. The stock market was drifting downward (heading for the big breakdown on May 26) and conservation of capital was the governing attitude. Possibly, I thought, a big Duesenberg could be an attractive and safe hedge against the hazy near future.

Our friendly verbal chess game continued. "Is there something definite I should know about?" I asked cautiously.

Putting his palm up like a traffic cop, he left the room for a moment, and came back with a gold-framed, 20 x 16, full-color artist's rendering of a bedazzling 1930 Duesenberg LeBaron Berline, a 4-door convertible sedan. I caught my breath as I held the stunning picture in my hands. This was one of the most desirable, the most resolve-destroying pictures of a car I had seen in a long time.

"Where is this gorgeous thing, and who owns it?" I asked in a muted voice.

"It's mine!" he replied, laughingly. "It's been in restoration for almost two years, and you're looking at what it will look like in a few months."

I pored over the painting, absorbing every magnificent detail. The color selection was outstanding; the main body panels were a honey beige, with fenders and body moldings of tobacco brown. Huge whitewall tires encircled the glittering chrome wire wheels, backed with orange painted brake drums. The body striping also was orange. He described the interior as having tobacco brown leather, and showed me a rich sample cutting. The carpets were going to be plush brown pile, and the top and trunk cover were to be fitted in California tan canvas. It was Bacchanalian, no less, and it made me dizzy with owner-itchings. The price was even more intoxicating, custom-made to order for a drunken roulette player.

Apparently my friend also uncomfortably recognized the humid financial climate and hastened to explain his position. "While my wife and I have dreamed about owning a Duesey ourselves someday, right now does not seem like the right time. After all, I'm in the business of selling cars, not keeping them!"

His expression of regret was also an open invitation to me to keep talking about the car. Just to think about it seriously, I told myself while my nervous system vibrated with excitement, was foolhardy, absurd, irrational. There wasn't any garage space for the giant. And then there was the huge cash figure to mull over. Perhaps there was another avenue to explore?

It occurred to me with a jolt. Tentatively, I put out feelers. Would he consider a trade involving my Rolls Royce as part payment? He fell into silence at this suggestion. He knew, as I did, that there were more potential buyers in the Rolls Royce class and price range than there were in the rarified Duesenberg atmosphere. This idea would hedge his own position, as well as give him some immediate cash.

While he was thinking, I was thinking heavily too. Firstly, I was a bit shocked at the callous sacrifice—offering my beloved Rolls—surprised at my treasonous and flighty changeability! What's gotten into me, I wondered, why would I do such a thing? Was the lure of the greatest name of them all so potent in itself, or was it some devastating competitive urge? My introspection was aborted in the next moment when he asked what figure I had in mind. I looked at the painting again, and the guilt feelings evaporated like a spot of dew in a noonday desert.

We guardedly theorized back and forth for a few moments, and soon arrived at a whopping number as a cash difference. All just conversation, I kept telling myself. On the basis of this general theory of relativity, I persuaded him to permit me to carry the picture home with me on loan, so that I could think about it further and confer with my wife. (This was similar to arrangements made between reputable jewel dealers, a sort of honor among thieves, to trust each other with diamonds on approval. But after all, it was *only* the picture.)

While flying home, I gathered quite a crowd about me on the plane as I held the work of art on my lap. The stewardesses crooned over the Duesey, while ignoring several crying babies in the aft cabin. I carried my trophy gently all the way home in the taxi, and burst through the front door of our home calling loudly for Bobbie. She ran down the stairs in her pajamas, and stood transfixed in the entry hall as I held the gorgeous picture in front of her nose.

"What's this?" she exclaimed comically.

"It's a picture of a Duesey, that's what it is—our Duesey!" I yelled back happily.

Awakened by the commotion, Bennett wandered sleepy-eyed out of his bedroom. His eyes popped. What excitement I brought home from that trip!

But it was not destined to be. Not yet, anyway. The next day was Saturday, and Arthur arrived about nine. He gulped when I showed him the masterpiece. Somehow I could feel his disapproval instantly, though he covered up with enthusiastic interest. I knew what was bugging him, and I could feel the same guilt-ridden mood in my family. We all really loved our gracious and wonderful Rolls, this was a disgraceful way to treat her! So what if she overheated?

Another event that same day contributed to the eventual, perhaps inevitable decision to leave well enough alone. A business associate of mine arrived for lunch, and became involved in the fracas. But now it was an open free-for-all.

"Alan," he said in amazement, "you've got to be nuts to trade that magnificent Rolls for another car of the same type, and add a small fortune on top of it!"

This was the cue for Bobbie to chime in with a mild opinion, and then Bennett got in the act. Arthur sat quietly munching his salad. I was touched

Another costume event with a grand old lady and a grand young lady.

and amazed to see the intensive loyalty for the Grand Old Lady, and it echoed my own secret sentiments precisely. Though not quite ready to make open avowal in the same vein, I knew that my problem of choice was duly finished, kaput, slaughtered in its infancy. I excused myself and walked out to the garage for a minute of reverence. Looking at my dear and magnificent phaeton, I realized that it was a heinous idea. She seemed, in my imagination, to glare back at me balefully, and I wondered how she would season my hash for even thinking such a thing possible. For sure she would find more than one way in the future to pay me back for my temporary lèse majesty. Oh well, I sighed, I deserve it.

Bobbie caught my eye as I came back to the dining room. "You can't do it, can you?" she asked softly.

I nodded humbly. All was well.

On Sunday, I made a ceremony (with a wrench in my belly) of packing the picture carefully, sorrowfully prepared to mail it back to Chicago on Monday. What hurt most was that this rare opportunity would most probably not be there at some future time, when circumstances might permit us to have both the Rolls and a Duesey together.

On Tuesday, I bought municipal bonds with my available cash, just to make sure.

POSTSCRIPTS BY MY WIFE
Young (Prince) Arthur galloped into our lives to see a Lamb; he stayed on, becoming a Lion in our garage arena. With a screwdriver as his sword and an oil drainpan as his shield, he attacked our nuisance problems of overheating,

Picnic in Matheson Hammock, Coral Gables, Florida, with champagne, Rolls Phantom, and two pretty passengers.

stalling, and slow-starting with patience and fortitude that warmed our hearts.

He grew into our lives as a friend, and then a co-aficionado, toying for hours over some small problem with the cars, or spending long evenings with Alan discussing their history, models, makes, designers, engines. Madame Rolly purred under his solicitous hands. (I call her that—not Princess or Duchess—because she is an American vintage Brewster-bodied Rolls, and therefore not of Royal blood, although she was often a Royal Nuisance with her stubborn ways.) We do love her something special, especially when we drive her out with her shiny polished aluminum bonnet, glinting chrome, manicured wire wheels, and her elegant black and fawn cloak. There's hardly a man who looks at her without smiling wistfully and saying, "Now that Lady is really something!"

I recall with a chuckle another time the Rolls quit stone dead on the way home from one of the shows. She had one of her coughing fits about 2 miles away from home base, and nothing we could do would get her started again (pre-Arthur Era). I headed home in a cab for a tow rope and the Riviera. By the time I got back Alan was in total despair. There sat the magnificent Rolls on the edge of a Negro community, and the little black children who'd never seen anything like it before were hovering about goggle-eyed. Trying to keep them from scratching his beauty had Alan frazzled. As I drove up I heard him say in vexation to a small, round-eyed, little boy, "Have you got just two cents? I'll give you this car for just two cents!" Fortunately, as the little fellow was reaching eagerly into his pocket, I was able to prevail upon Alan to tie the rope to the frame of the Riviera, or who knows what might have happened! We then ingloriously paraded our way (no, slunk our way) home along a back street route we had figured out in advance, so as not to be seen. But the neighbors saw us—there was no other way down our street.

It was after that incident that I feel Alan first began to think about trading her off, even after Arthur cured the trouble.

I suspect the short "aberration" with the Chicago Duesenberg partially stemmed from dimly-remembered events of that nature!

15

Big Red

 In mid-May, I had to make a sudden business trip to Atlanta. I had heard about a large and great private European Classic car collection through a friend in that city. Arrangements were set up to make the visit, and I was picked up early one evening and driven out to see this unusual and rare group of cars. The twenty highly-restored automobiles were housed on the estate in a specially built red-brick garage, which had garage doors all around the structure so that each car faced its own roll-up exit. This was the ultimate concept I had ever seen in housing a collection. I thought wistfully of the ease and convenience of being able to drive any car in and out without moving any other car. The garage also had a complete workshop, and the whole place was totally air-conditioned from wall to wall. My friend told me in an aside that the price tag on this "storage" building was over $60,000.

After digesting this sanguine bit of information, I started wandering about in the dazzling agglomeration of cars. On a far larger scale than myself, the owner had specialized in restoring open-model European marques: racers, phaetons, tourers, and convertibles gleamed under the closely-spaced florescent lights. A great and massive 540K "A" type roadster was the lead car in the ménage, augmented by two Rolls Royces, a Lagonda tourer of exquisite proportions, an Isotta-Fraschini with its impressive bulk and grandeur, a sweeping Delahaye boattail roadster, two Aston-Martin racers, one a boattail; an SS-100 pre-Jaguar, a black and silver Horch convertible, and other rare treasures of similar stature. It was difficult to absorb quickly, as most of the cars were top-prize winners to boot.

One exciting American car stood lonely but unabashed amid this connoisseur splendor in a small alcove off to one side, as though shunned for being a domestic vintage. This car, a gorgeous red 1936 Auburn "852" boattail Speedster, was a blatant inconsistency in the European collection. Somehow, I was pleased to learn that it might be for sale, for this very reason. My own collector's rules and confines did not preclude this car being a strong contender for my affections. I had carried a bag for one since the age of sixteen, and Bobbie and I had often cast sheep's eyes at this splendid type at many a car show. It was also one of the most sought-after motorcars of our times, and I knew he was aware of that fact, too. Over the years it had gained enormous prestige, having been designed by the renowned Gordon Buehrig, of Duesenberg fame. It was alleged that the designer considered it one of his greatest classic concepts, and justly so.

This same body style had also been built on Duesenberg and Cord chassis, but its major exploitation had been with the Auburn Straight-8 Lycoming aircraft-type engine. In its day the Speedster had been the penultimate plaything of wealthy sportsmen and gay blades; as a two-seater it left much to be desired for general use (as we discovered on many occasions later). But it was beautiful, breathtaking, and swashbuckling, like no other car of its era.

My host sensed my gourmet alimentary rumblings. A rapid examination (just skimming over the surface) showed up a number of obvious minor troubles: paint nicks, poor chrome, worn carpeting, but nothing serious. The wire wheels were in need of repainting, but worst of all was the cosmetic appearance of the engine. Although completely mechanically rebuilt in the recent past, it had never been refinished to match its mechanical condition. It was rusty, grimy, and dirty, and a few cracked wires showed that some electrical work might also be on the docket. The body lacquer itself was excellent with the exception of a scratch here and there, and I concluded that a couple of months of applied effort would bring her back to top rate condition throughout, and make her a high-point winner. The tires were almost brand new, big whitewall Martin-Cords, another minor factor in my interest.

The owner caught the signal. We started dickering rather casually, my opening comments being that the car was also out of my field. As a super-purist, he wanted to move it out of his European collection, and we hung on this point for a few minutes. His price was high—there was a definite known market value on the boattail Speedster—and I searched for the right solution

Big Red. The famous Auburn chrome exhausts, rakish torpedo fenders, and headlights blend into the tapered boattail with perfection.

for both of us. Suddenly a possibility occurred to me. I told him about my 1952 Mercedes-Benz 300-D convertible sedan.

His ears pointed. "I've always had a yen for a 300 for personal use," he exclaimed to my delight. We had a deal started.

In trading one car for another with the cash difference as the fulcrum, the leverage has to be applied cautiously. I agreed to send photos and complete details of the Mercedes, and we left it at that. They were sent out immediately upon my return, and a few days later we started telephone negotiations, rapidly reaching an accord. We now had to work out the physical transfer of the cars, and it was arranged that I would drive the Mercedes up to North Florida, just below the Georgia line, and that he would bring the Auburn from Atlanta to that halfway spot. We were to meet at a Holiday Inn at a specified exit off the expressway. The appointment was set for 8:00 A.M., on Saturday of the Memorial Day weekend. I phoned Arthur to invite him along for the long drive, and he accepted with alacrity. This promised to be a lark. We departed about 11:00 A.M. on Friday in bright sunshine, in high spirits, and equipped with food basket, drinks and good wishes.

The Mercedes, with its capacious seats and luxurious fittings, was a real pleasure to drive on that long trip. I had never before had it out on tour; it behaved so superbly that more than once I felt small nagging regrets about the deal. Here was a great modern classic automobile that was perfect for "daily use," and it was on its way to be traded for another haughty primadonna that rightfully expected to be garaged constantly, primped, pampered and prepared for "show only." I consoled myself during this vacillating mood with the memory of thrilling adolescent dreams of owning a boattail Speedster. This rationale worked, and I was then able to relax and enjoy the trip.

We spotted an angry mass of black storm clouds in the north, and this gave us a diverting game to play with the winding parkway, now angling away from the thunderhead, then swooping back to a line on its dead center. For awhile it looked as though we might skirt around the southern edge of the storm, but then the road would take a wide westerly swing through the hills of the orange grove country. There was nothing at all we could do about it; it was like a roulette wheel, out of our control but fun to play. A wide easterly turn headed us right back to center, and suddenly we were right in the middle of the huge torrential rainstorm. Wipers flicking madly, we slowed to a crawl; a huge tractor-trailer raced past us, drenching the car in its flying wake, and a solid sheet of water splattered through the slightly open driver's window, soaking Arthur, who was at the wheel at the time. At the same moment the left windshield wiper died, and Arthur had his hands full guiding the Mercedes to the side of the road through the teeming downpour. The waterfall drummed on the canvas roof as we sat there helplessly. It was quite impossible to get out of the car for repairs.

We waited patiently for the torrent to abate, and when it let up enough, Arthur jumped out to fix the wiper. To do this, he planned first to open the trunk, grab a raincoat, get the tools, open the hood, and go like hell to beat the resuming downpour. But it caught him in his shirtsleeves before he could locate the raincoat. Half-soaked, he quickly found an errant nut which had slipped loose from the wiper-arm, swiftly made the repair, and bolted back into the car, pulling off his wet shirt on the way in. He drove bare-chested, wiper working fine all the way, until we made it to the next rest stop.

Our second incident on this tour de force occurred on a 45-mile stretch between exits or gas stations. The fuel gauge, which had registered ample gas on the previous dry-up rest stop, unaccountably fell below the quarter mark in one swoop, without any warning. We anxiously began to do mathematical calculations, and disconcertingly came up with the barest possibility of making the required distance to the next station. Since we now were almost midway between exits, it was impractical to go backward, and we had visions of sitting helplessly on the parkway in the storm, between nowhere and noplace, waiting for help. We worriedly tried to guess at the best economy speed range as the needle inexorably fell toward the empty mark. We semi-coasted along, accelerating only for hills, nursing our gas. The red warning light nervously flickered on and off to add to our discomfort. We had about five miles to go; the red light was steady, the needle quivering right on the empty line. We watched anxiously through the streaming windshield for a road decline—and there it was, downhill all the way, as we passed the welcome sign, "Rest Stop, 2 miles Ahead." Coaxing, mentally pushing, we rolled into the ramp of the gas station as the engine died about 200 feet from the pumps. We got out and pushed the rest of the way.

These events were to be the keynote of the whole round trip! We arrived at the appointed place about dinner time with no further incident. The rain had stopped, the air was clear and pure, and we congratulated ourselves on the successful completion of phase 1. After dinner, we washed the car and emptied our personal gear. In the trunk we discovered about 6 inches of water in the deep side recess. This was a peculiar mystery; apparently the deep water pockets we had pounded through, often over the hubcaps, had forced splash entry somewhere under the trunk panel and flooded the lower section. Arthur looked at me unhappily and barked, "Your camera was down in that well!" He reached down and pulled out my sopping new 35MM import automatic. Chalk up our first real casualty.

"The hell with that," I grunted, "the cashier's check is down there too, in the pocket of my coat!"

We grabbed the soaked mass and pulled out the envelope. The check was dog-eared and limp, but it was still readable, and good currency. We hung it on a paper clip all night, in front of the air conditioner, to dry.

At 8:05 the next morning, there was a punctual knock at our door. Two bedraggled men peered at us through red-rimmed eyes; the Auburn had been driven through the night from Atlanta, also in driving rain, with the top down all the way! We shook hands, laughing, and I glanced out across the parking lot, heart leaping at the sight of the tapered boattail shimmering red in the early sunlight. This was the great moment—it was all worth it! How many times have we felt that way?

We were all in a rush to get started on the long trips back, so our paperwork was concluded rapidly, crinkled check and all. Having never seen the Mercedes, he was anxious for his first look. We went outside, and I asked why they had driven all night with the top down, in the rain. Sheepishly, they admitted that it took some effort to install the Auburn special top devices, and it had seemed easier to just keep going. "Besides," one said convincingly, "the rakish angle of the windshield deflected the rain right over the cockpit." Except for gas stops, they said they'd had no problem.

Arthur and I decided we'd better see for ourselves what was involved in this top installation. I remembered hearing that the Speedster sports tops were stored separately in the tail and required some special treatment in mooring all the snaps and clamps. The four of us together fussed about for a few minutes. Arthur and I got the hang of it without too much trouble, and installed it snugly. This elicited a further bit of reluctant information. "With the top on, it gets pretty hot in the car," we were told by the owner. "There are a few small holes in the exhaust pipes, and that throws quite a bit of heat into the cockpit!"

This was our first disconcerting clue about an extensive exhaust system rebuild we were going to need immediately, but we had no idea at that moment just how massive this job was going to be. (They didn't know yet about the water in the Mercedes trunk either!)

Meanwhile, Arthur was giving the Auburn the once-over. He called out a question. "What's this gouge in the right front fender?"

"Oh, that," the owner said debonairly, "happened in a gas station when we got a little too close to the pump. By the way," he added, "watch out for those wide torpedo fenders, they're pretty bulbous!"

I felt it only fair then to explain that the Mercedes used a little oil at high speeds. Even-Steven! What other cunning secrets awaited us in the Auburn? What had we forgotten to mention about the M-B? We packed our gear into the boattail and drove away. They followed us right up on the parkway, took the northbound ramp, and we waved goodbye to each other as the Auburn headed south.

Once on the road, it didn't take us very long to understand why they had driven it topless through the long wet night. The heat coming up through the floorboards was red-hot, and the monoxide fumes were suffocating. Those gorgeous and celebrated exposed chrome-plated exhausts on the left side of the car blew a forced billow of heat right at the driver like a blast furnace, so we shortly decided to remove the canvas roof and stow it in the tail. After this was accomplished, the discomfort was confined to hot feet only, and our face and body purple flushes receded as the wind blew into the cockpit. With over 350 miles to go, we settled down to serious driving and began to glory in the excitement of this powerful demon. People in passing cars whistled and waved—the boattail was really something to see. With only a scattered handful left in existence, and almost all of them in Concours

Some Horseless Carriage! All cars over 35 years old get this license plate in Florida.

condition safely stowed in garages, perhaps some realized that they were being offered a rare chef d'oeuvre.

I began to feel a strange click and slight wobble in the left front wheel. We were traveling about 60 miles per hour, really loafing for the Auburn, and enjoying it immensely. But this oddity soon had my guard up, and I shifted gears up and down while experimenting with the brake pedal to determine what was wrong. I mentioned it to Arthur, and we agreed that we'd better get off at the next exit to have a look. On the way down the exit ramp, at low speed, the wobble became more pronounced, and, suspecting the very worst, I rolled into the gas station luckily located at the bottom of the ramp. As we came to a stop, there was a heavy thump, and the Auburn laid over with an abrupt lurch. Our left front wheel had fallen completely off the axle, and the car was hanging on the perimeter of the tire, which had most fortunately become wedged under the fender at a crazy 45-degree angle!

In shock and astonishment, we leapt out of the car. An attendant, mouth agape, stammered, "Migod. Your w-wheel f-fell off!"

Other motorists from other cars in the station walked over, shaking their heads in disbelief—here was this stunning showpiece, crippled, but miraculously unharmed. It made the mind boggle to consider what could have happened on the expressway at sixty miles an hour.

Arthur and I looked at each other blankly, still in mild shock. "Somebody up there likes us," he said in a weak voice. I noticed vaguely that my formerly overheated feet were ice cold.

Still shaking, we made a hurried inspection. We pulled the hubcap, and found to our anger and disgust that there had been only three lugs out of five on the wheel to begin with, and that of the three, two were stripped of threading. Our first angry reaction was that we could have been killed by this carelessness or neglect, but then again, to be fair, who would ever think to look at wheel lugs under ordinary circumstances? The sympathetic gas station owner allowed us to rummage through his parts drawers and boxes, and we were overjoyed to find half a dozen truck lugs that perfectly fitted holes in the wheel. Two were slightly too long, and these were filed down to size. The front end of the car was raised, the wheel was locked on tightly with the truck lugs, and then, just to be sure, we completely lifted the Auburn on jacks at both ends, and removed and inspected every lug on the other three wheels. One other showed up badly worn and was replaced. About an hour and a half after we had plopped into the station, we drove out secure in the knowledge that at least in this one respect, we would have no further emergency. The next few miles our cautious driving was a bit unsteady, but it was no fault of the car, only the still-quivering drivers. We were also kept moist and cool from then on, as it rained intermittently all day on the way to Miami. Hooded by our raincoats, and huddled down in the seats, we plugged on doggedly.

Our trouble-beset odyssey continued. We had discovered early on the trip that the gas gauge wasn't functioning at all and as we had no idea of the rate of gas consumption, we stopped frequently for gas fill-ups. This gave us some rough form of measure, and we pegged it at about 12 miles per gallon to play safe. We prepared a mathematical chart of tank capacity vs. miles driven, and this was our gasoline gauge. It worked fine, until we got careless during a period of sangfroid with the car, somewhere about halfway between the

Stuart and Palm Beach exits, a gap of about 35 miles between service stations. During this period, the sun came out warmly, and with it, our hot-foot treatment was reinstated. But we were having a ball, joking and immensely intrigued with the restoration plans for the rare and glamorous Speedster, and we totally forgot to do our arithmetic in the long stretch. Without a burp or a warning gasp, the Auburn started sucking air, and we were lucky to have enough momentum to drift to a stop in the welcome concrete shade of an overpass. We looked at each other lamely, and, without even a word, I got out and started begging for a ride on the busy expressway. I stuck my thumb out pleadingly for 10 minutes, but the fast-moving traffic went by with hardly a glance. Where were all our admirers then?

The object, of course, was to get to the nearest gas station at the next southward exit, about 15 miles down the road, try to commandeer a gas can, and somehow get back to the Auburn the same day. Another ten minutes of begging and cussing finally worked its hex on a black Porsche. The driver looked us over in amazement, and said he'd be glad to get me to the nearest station. Little did we realize that the Memorial Day weekend was hardly the best time for finding help in the sleepy Florida countryside.

Every gas station beyond the exit for about five miles on the country road was closed for the holiday. I started to feel deeply embarrassed. My driver-host was genial enough but I could see he hadn't bargained for an all-day trip, polite as he was. I was getting ready to ask him to drop me then and there when we came to a whistle-stop crossroads, with a gas station on each of the four corners. Luckily, one was open, but it was already five o'clock (we had expected to be home in Coconut Grove by *four*) and they were locking the pumps as we drove in. The southern pork-chopper type hasn't much use for big city folks, particularly in fancy sports cars, so it was quite a struggle to convince them to unhook the lock and chain and fill a five-gallon can. At a dollar a gallon, I finally convinced them of the wisdom of this decision, and I didn't complain about the dented and rusty can either.

Thanking my savior in the Porsche who sailed away thankfully, I then faced the problem of getting back to the Auburn, about 20 miles north. An enterprising chap in a big straw hat, who was leaning indolently against an old pickup truck, divined my plight. "I'll take you as far as the tollgate for two dollars," he offered.

"It's a deal," I replied without hesitation.

The tollgate guard became my next hurdle in the obstacle course. "No hitchhiking allowed at the gate," he warned severely. "You'll have to go up the road a piece, and wait there for a lift."

Lugging the forty pound gas can, I took off at a trot, breathing hard in the heat, and sighted two cars entering the head of the toll lane. Both cars went by my disheveled person without a glance. I prepared myself for a long hot summer. About ten minutes later a startling-looking rig hove into sight. Thumbing vigorously, I flagged them down. It was a battered old Ford sedan, pulling an even more battered Ford stock car racer on a trailer. I explained my predicament, and they said sure, hop in. Our conversation naturally turned to cars, and I know they thought I was kidding when I told them about the Auburn; I think they expected to deliver me to a flivver. Were they surprised to see the gleaming red bullet across the road! I invited them to come over for a look and we all crossed the road dodging the zooming traffic. These good guys refused my proffered five-dollar bill. They said it was enough reward just to see the beautiful Speedster.

A few minutes later, with no start-up difficulty, we were on our way again with a zoom and a roar. It was now about 6:30 P.M., time for dinner and phone calls home to the waiting families. We pulled in to the next rest area and parked the brilliant red torpedo in front of the Hot Shoppe restaurant. A crowd of tourists instantly gathered around the car, so we had to eat in separate shifts, standing guard duty against the curious kids and their even more curious dads. By the time we left, it was starting to sprinkle again, and within a few miles the deluge caught us. The rain cooled the car, but we were weary and numb from the day's sun and engine heat, the long drive, and the unforeseen difficulties and delays. We were only forty miles from home, and though it had really been a grueling two days, we somehow floated into a free-flight mood of hilarity. We had it made, we thought, and in relief our jubilant conversation went something like this:

Arthur: Who else ever had a car with full shower facilities and foot warming equipment?
Alan: That's not all! How about the horizontal water stream to keep you cool at chest level? (This reference was to the leaky rubber gaskets between cowl and windshield frame that permitted the driving rain to fly straight into the cockpit.)
Arthur: I wonder how we can show these unique features to the judges for extra show points?

Alan: I don't think the judges would be impressed. (Childish laughter by both.)

Arthur: How about this: Maybe we can install a pair of tanks under the instrument panel to catch the rain, then with a spigot in each, we can have a regular supply of scotch and water.

Alan: Uh-uhn. Drunken driver problems. But how about a seltzer-maker, with fruit syrup in the other tank. Or you could have 2¢ plain.

(More punch-drunk laughter, to the point of tears.)

Arthur: There should be some way to convert the exhaust heat for baking pies. Then we could have pie and hot tea, with floating tea bags in the tanks.

This was too much for us in our weakened mental state. We had to pull over to the side of the road, heaving and wheezing in the slashing downpour, covered with our raincoat-tents; we laughed until the tension-relieving mood dribbled away. Wiping our eyes, and not daring to look at each other, we switched seats and started up again. It was almost twilight as we drove out of the cloud bank into the late sunshine. Suddenly, my blue lightweight dungaree sailing cap flew off my head. By the time we could stop, it was already 500 feet behind us on the grassy slope beside the expressway. I ran back for the cap, just as a State Trooper spotted us. He crossed over the median, pulled in behind us, and strolled over pompously, sizing up the rare beauty. "No parking on the apron except for repairs," he said threateningly.

At this stage, in no mood to care much about anything, I said, in a jocular tone, "Where were *you* when we ran out of gas?"

Arthur and I, still hung over from our hilarious mood, started laughing again.

He looked at us queerly. I don't think he appreciated the joke, which he proved by pulling his ticket pad out of his jacket. "What's wrong with you guys?" he growled.

I put my hand on his arm. "Wait a minute, officer," I said, still snorting a little. "How would you like to forget about the ticket, and trade your nice Ford for this genuine valuable Classic?"

He pushed back his trooper's campaign hat, looked at us wonderingly with his hands on his hips, squinted his eyes, and retorted, "How would you chaps like to spend the night in the genuine clink?"

The time had clearly arrived for serious explanations. I told him how the cap had flown off in the wind, I told him about our wheel incident, and running out of gas. I threw in a little about the rain, the exhaust heat and the

Mercedes trip the day before. He relaxed. "And you want me to trade a new Ford for one of these crazy cars?" he asked. We knew then that we had found a friend.

He began to enjoy the chance meeting. "It isn't common to stop a pair of nuts in a prize like this," he continued good-humoredly, "I think my buddies would like to see it too, back at the ranch." We knew he was kidding now, so I gave him a short-order course in car collecting and restoration. He listened in fascination. We opened the engine hood and let him poke around, answering all his questions.

Before he left the scene he admonished us to be careful. "Night's coming on, and I'll bet your lights are not too great, and there's lots of holiday traffic." With a friendly wave and a headshake, he took off, a convert to the cause.

We started off again in the deepening twilight. Had we ever thought to check the headlights? Had we thought we'd be on the road this late? We hit the switch. Only one headlight was working, and it was a brownish color at that! We pulled off the road again and tried to open the other headlight casing, but this bullet-shaped mystery was not about to yield its secret on such short notice. In irritation, Arthur gave the headlight a few hard whacks, and the light kicked on. We were now about twenty miles from our seemingly unreachable goal. We decided that, come what may, we were not going to stop again of our own volition, so long as the Auburn held out and the flesh was willing. With the left headlight popping on and off, and the other one furnishing about two candlepower, we crept along in the holiday-returning nighttime traffic, the engine inferno belching fury into our faces. At 9:15 we drove into the courtyard of my home.

You may well ask, as we did: How *can* it be worth it? Try it—you'll see!

POSTSCRIPTS BY MY WIFE
In our life with the cars, they come and they go. I said goodbye to "Fräulein Merzedes" without a tear. She was another of our D.U.C.'s originally meant for Alan to use and enjoy. Once I found out what a great ferryboat she made, by now you know who drove her most of the time. She was a handsome old Walkyrie, and I got a lot of pleasure driving her about for the routine chores.

What was best for me was that she had a reserve gas tank. Whenever I ran low (as I often do) there was always that dependable reserve tank to switch over with a flick of a lever. Too bad Alan and Arthur didn't remember about that—or had I ever mentioned it? —they wouldn't have had to push her to the gas tanks. And that was a lot of car to push!

They were certainly safe in driving her upstate. But I was a bit worried about the trip back with the unknown Auburn, though I knew that whatever came up they would work it out. But who would have ever figured on a wheel coming off? Then when it got to be around dinnertime, I began to worry a little, even realizing the holiday traffic would hold them up a bit. I was real happy to get the phone call a little while later, and without Alan going into detail I could tell they'd had some awful experiences that day.

It was good to hear them finally pull into the drive. We all rushed out to look her over, and I must admit that glowing red hull was a sight to see in the courtyard spotlights.

So one car departed, and another returned in its place, and we were still running a total of seven. How I'm looking forward to the day we have two!

16

The Side-Mount Car

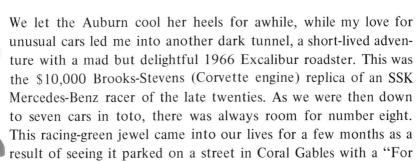

We let the Auburn cool her heels for awhile, while my love for unusual cars led me into another dark tunnel, a short-lived adventure with a mad but delightful 1966 Excalibur roadster. This was the $10,000 Brooks-Stevens (Corvette engine) replica of an SSK Mercedes-Benz racer of the late twenties. As we were then down to seven cars in toto, there was always room for number eight. This racing-green jewel came into our lives for a few months as a result of seeing it parked on a street in Coral Gables with a "For Sale" sign and a phone number on the windshield. This was another of those tidbits I had long had on my automobile-mania Wanted List. I had seen them flash by me, taunting me in the Ferrari, and, gambling glutton that I am, I tried the auto crap table again. I phoned the number and made a low bid for this 4-year-old contemporary classic. It was turned down. I left my number. Behold! A few weeks later my price was accepted by the disillusioned Key West dentist, who had had his fill. (No pun intended.) This little two-seater marvel, built of fiberglas and aluminum on a tight, short chassis, boasts a Corvette 327 "souped up" like the vats in Campbell's Kitchens! On each side, three flashy chrome exhausts leap out of the engine bonnet; they are actually air breathers, allowing the carburetors to function at maximum efficiency.

There are no doors in the body, so getting into the tight cockpit requires throwing one leg over the low-slung side-panel, pulling the other leg in beside it, and gently lowering the body into the seat, while hanging onto the windshield. (If anyone knows a better way to do it, I'd like to hear about it.) Every time I had to do this, I fervently wished I could temporarily shrink to four feet, nine inches. And I won't go into detail about the windshield almost tearing off the cowl as you lowered away.

During the training period with this filly, in one of my heaving self-removals from the play-pen cockpit, the steering wheel almost *did* come off in my hands. Arthur soon discovered that the main nut on the steering column was faulty, and fixed that dangerous condition without delay. As he had already become deeply involved in reconditioning the Auburn, several other needed items went unheeded on the Excalibur.

We had named the boattail "Big Red," after squeezing it into the garage next to the Rolls, by usurping the position of the Aston-Martin. The shifting of cars that took place whenever we brought a new addition into the family usually required a strategy conference with all executives on tap. The majority vote is what put the Aston in the carport, replacing the Ferrari, which had replaced the Lamborghini, which had replaced the Mercedes. As a result, the Ferrari was relegated to the lowly location of the canopy on the other side of the house. To make room for the Excalibur, the MG-K was driven over to Arthur's house to await future developments. She was a good-natured little baby, and never complained about the neglectful passing over of her needs, time and again.

While we developed our theories about the big rebuilding job of the exhaust system on Big Red, which was first on the agenda, I played around with the new toy Excalibur, and rapidly came to one rigid conclusion. Bobbie was never going to drive this green slithering reptile. Why? Well, one of the first times I bolted up our curved, test-tracky street (the neighbors sometimes shake their fists at me, and one once threw a whole grapefruit, right off his tree) I must have been thinking I was driving the Ferrari because I had a big surprise waiting. I was shocked almost insensible when the rear end lunged out sideways at me as I skidded around the number one bend. Did you ever see the rear of your car facing you from the *side,* while you're looking at it from the driver's seat? That may be an exaggeration, but that's how it felt momentarily. I foggily decided that it must be a driver error, and never tried it again. Obviously this was not a Ferrari; I guessed the rear traction didn't equal the engine torque. Taking those S-curves in my belching 330 GTC was always a cinch, and really had me spoiled for lesser machinery, which covers just about all other automobiles made.

Having to treat the replica SSK with diffidence was a bit disappointing, but truly what can you expect for a mere ten grand? On the straightaway the thrust was entirely secure, though quite deafening. I needed to figure out

Squat and menacing: the Excalibur. Note chrome side-breathers, leather strap on bonnet, trumpet horns, and motorcycle-type fenders.

how to get places without dependable cornering, but this of course was only a matter of choice. Another thing to watch out for was keeping away from the sizzling hot, side-mounted chrome mufflers. We all have had blisters on our shins for this lapse of memory. Try getting out of the cockpit after a flying run without having one leg catch you on the way out and lay up to the scorching metal. Football shin guards may be the only answer. To top off the gregarious qualities of this Excalibur, installing the vinyl swivel top in the rain makes the Auburn installation look like kid's play. It's much easier to pull in under a tree or a portico and simply wait it out.

One day I took Bobbie and Bennett for a ride in a new development where the streets were not yet fully paved. I floored the accelerator pedal in a moment of abandon, hit a slightly uneven manhole cover mound, and almost lost the two of them in mid-air above the car, as they had forgotten to clip on their seat belts! Luckily, their impetus, floating above the seats, matched the speed of the car (Newton or Einstein?) and they plopped back, out of breath. That was the day I decided to sell the sexy vampire. There were seven calls on the first ad, and they were all panting with eagerness to part with their money, almost as much as I was to part with the car. I got out of that one, with a whole skin, breaking even, physically and financially. Maybe I'm getting too old for such experiments.

Our plans for the important Auburn work were now completely drawn up, and we jumped into the ring with both feet. We knew it was going to be a great heavyweight fight, and we knew who was destined to be the winner. But it was sure to be a full fifteen-rounder. With Excalibur out of the way and the MG-K in the deep freeze again, we could concentrate on the big Auburn jobs over the summer, finish up the Rolls detailing, and be ready with both cars for the big AACA Regional meet, again at Pier 66, at the end of October, 1970.

We began jabbing away at the guts of the boattail by pulling the chrome-flex tubes off the exhausts, and were horrified to see the tremendous extent of the rotting-out, the huge holes, and the open cracks along the entire length of two of the four exhaust pipes. It was easy to see why the heat had been so fierce. With the crumbling pipes as samples, I started to hunt for a custom pipe-bender. This was quite an assignment in Miami, but I finally found one shop able to handle the intricate twists and bends, though even they were doubtful about the end result. They agreed to give it a try—but with no responsibility on their part. Take pot luck, they said, at $125 for the final result, come what may. We got lucky; on Saturday I handed my prized black pretzels to Arthur, feeling like a small boy proudly presenting his first frog to his mother. First he sighed with relief, and then he blew out an anxious breath. "I hope we don't have to pull off the fender to get these in place," he said dolefully.

Our first task was to loosen the entire muffler and tailpipe assembly under the car, pushing it back out of the way to allow jam-in space for connecting the new contortions to the good existing sections. While Arthur bitterly cursed the unyielding rusted clamps and bolts, I started wrapping the new pipe units with eighth-inch thick asbestos cloth. This burly tapelike material then had to be spiralled with stainless steel wire to prevent scrunching up as the flexible chrome covers were forced back over the wrapped pipes. I found it almost impossible to hold onto the weird shapes—they seemed to have a life of their own, wriggling, rolling over, and falling out of my lap with every spiral turn of the asbestos and wire.

It took me four hours to complete the set, which also included three of us in a taffy-pulling contest, stepping all over each other while pushing the chrome-cover flex tubes back over the newly wrapped pipes. Never, never again! I swore. But who commercially would do such a job? More than once I put a voodoo on the former owner—a few little holes indeed!

We were now ready to fight them through the cutouts in the front left fender, and hook them up to the main exhaust line under the car. This was the fifteenth round, and it was still a standoff fight. When I say fight, I mean battle, wage war, charge into the fray, outflank the enemy, frontal assault, rear skirting attack, flank movement, pincer ploy; *Battle of the Bulge, El Alamein, Iwo Jima;* Pershing, Patton and Eisenhower!

Battered, grimy, cut, bruised, sweaty, and panting with vengeful satisfaction, we stood back, the winner, just after midnight of that memorable day. The bloodied garage floor was covered with crippled tools, mutilated buckets and rags, mangled drop cloths. This was one private war to be recorded in the Pentagon Archives.

With this victory behind us, we gained confidence and a full head of steam. After all, what could faze us now? Long lists were clipped up on the work board. It seemed there were endless jobs to be done. I recalled with a vengeful tug of emotion that this car had been advertised as "mechanically perfect and in show condition" a couple of months before I bought it, but in a forgiving spirit, Arthur and I agreed that the previous owner may either not have realized how many problems there were, or simply did not have our sense of perfection. Privately, I only bought that theory partially.

Our next attack plan was general. Door plates needed to be rebuilt to keep the doors from rattling, handles needed new pins and inner springs. Bumper brackets and iron mounting pads had to be completely reshaped and refitted. All engine accessories such as starter, carburetor, generator, distributor, etc., were to be dismantled, rebuilt, and repainted in black enamel. All other small items such as coil, oil filter tank, air filter, were also to be removed, overhauled, and resprayed. We had no way of knowing if these jobs had been done, so rather than guess and be sorry later, we tore them all out. It proved to be a very wise decision, as every piece was corroded and gooked-up. Again, I remembered the assurances that she was "mechanically perfect." We ran into trouble with the horns, so they were both removed, resonator

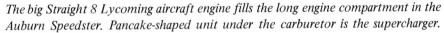

The big Straight 8 Lycoming aircraft engine fills the long engine compartment in the Auburn Speedster. Pancake-shaped unit under the carburetor is the supercharger.

mechanisms rebuilt, and the graceful two-foot long trumpets chrome-plated.

With all the small parts out of the way, the entire engine block was easily open for painting with the authentic green engine enamel used in these cars originally. Arthur also dropped the lower drip pans, straightened the kinked sheet metal, and repainted them black. Happily, the undercarriage had been excellently done, but we couldn't really understand why this was so, while the engine compartment had been allowed to fall into such disrepute.

In the driver's compartment, the lists included rebuilding the wipers—they had struggled weakly on the trip downstate—and having them replated. The massive windshield posts and upper frames were totally removed for plating and new glass. To our continuing distress this required removal of the inside leather liners under the instrument panel to allow us to get at the securing bolts, and, while we were at it, we saw that it would be best to pull the instrument panel to allow relacquering of the red metal background. On the panel itself, we had to replace the radio dial face, and Arthur was forced to reproduce the red-and-white selector needle when none was to be found anywhere.

Someday I'm going to ask him to make me an egg. He'll probably ask, "From what kind of bird?"

Throughout and overall, every possible piece of chrome that could be removed was removed, including the bumpers, taillights, hinges, knobs, top brace fittings, rear window frame, and hundreds of small exposed screws in the firewall, dash panel, and door panels. We even found some hold-down screws in the carpeting that were taken to the platers. Keeping track of these minute parts was a diligent chore in itself with duplicate lists carefully recorded, and locked away. These minute details and major measures might indicate that the car was seriously deficient in overall condition, but this was not the case. The real motivation for all these meticulous attentions was simply that a great, rare "852" Speedster should get the best of everything, even to the redoing of a bumper with only a few scattered pinpoint pit-marks. No, let us not malign Big Red; blame only our unappeasable appetite to make her as near-perfect as humanly possible.

In pulling the chrome, we naturally also removed the important three-dimensional SUPER—CHARGED plaques on each side of the hood. These 16" long plates were fairly well preserved, but not really sharp, so off to the plater's they went with the boxes full of other gadgets. No particular special attention was given to these plates, it seemed like a pretty routine plating assignment. A couple of days after the delivery of the big batch of stuff to the plating house, I was given a terse message by my secretary, ominous in portent, to come right over to the shop which was just around the corner. After years of harmonious relationship with these fine people, this was a most unusual request. Having done all the chrome on my cars from the Alvis onward, I trusted them completely. For their part, I was a unique customer in their big commercial operation, with interesting gadgets and specialties that enlivened their rather humdrum routine assignments. My chrome plating work was so special that we jointly gave it a Hollywood kind of name, "Radcliff's Blue Diamond." It was often their pleasure, and mine too, to attend local shows and listen with glee to other collectors exclaim over the superior blue-point dazzle reflections in the sunlight.

So, when I walked in that day to see their crestfallen faces, I knew that something horrible must have occurred. Bernie, the chief Guru, an artist in his own right, silently handed me one of the "SUPER–CHARGED" plates, heartbreak showing in his eyes.

"I don't know what happened, Alan," he said in bewilderment. "Right under my nose these things burnt up in the acid-etching tank. I didn't even have time to yank them out it happened so fast!"

He handed me the two charred, eaten-out strips, blackened, full of holes, and burnt right through the raised letters. "Man, oh man," I said softly, "what do we do now?"

The search for replacements began at once, by phone and mail. My prime hope was that there'd be a pair at the San Francisco "A-C-D" parts depot, but their answer was negative. I tried the Speedster replica builder in Broken Arrow, Oklahoma. He was having trouble himself, he said, getting them for his special production Speedsters. However, he advised that he was planning to make a mold for casting, and might have them available in a few months. It was too late for that, the AACA show was less than a month away. More letters were mailed. It seemed that there were none in the woodwork, in the United States, or in heaven, where they were probably made originally.

Arthur looked at the pair of destroyed plates contemplatively. "There's only one thing to do," he whispered in his simplistic, clear-minded way. "We'll have to have a new pair *made*."

This statement was so amazing, I could only gasp, "By whom?" My voice felt like it was up about three octaves.

"By me, of course, Alan," he said quietly.

I shook my head emphatically, "That's impossible," I said flatly, remembering some of my previous thoughts. "How can you make an egg?"

"You got any better ideas?" he asked humorously. You gotta' admit, he had me there!

Unbelievably about one week later, he presented me with a small white pasteboard jeweler's box. Inside on a cushion of white absorbent cotton lay an exquisite set of letters, S-U-P-E-R-C-H-A-R-G-E-D. They were cut from one-eighth-inch thick copper plate to the exact stylized configuration of the original letters, and polished like jeweled pins. I sat down with a thump, rolling my eyes theatrically in my head in total incredulity. I was also deeply touched and grateful, and from that moment on, I viewed him with new and even more personal affection and respect.

The rest was duck soup. He finished the second set the following week, along with the two brass mounting plates, beveled to the same rolled edge of the originals, with even the screw-bosses silver-soldered to the back side. The cutout letters went to the platers (to their astonishment and joy) one set at a time, for individual chroming. When completed Arthur mounted them letter by letter to the chromed back plates, spacing them to micrometer perfection. We have been told by experts that our pair of "S" plates are the finest in the world. Why not, with 80 hours of meticulous craftsmanship and love lavished upon them?

I have always dimly wondered if Arthur flew up to Tiffany's to have them made up.

We continued on through the welter of lists, working through the beastly hot Florida summer. We finally found a way to air-condition the garage, in a manner of speaking, by opening the entry door into a corridor in the house, deflecting the grille blades in the hall ceiling and sucking the cool air out by fan. This helped us eat our way through the huge red restoration cheese, bite-by-bite. First, the engine components were replaced on the freshly painted block, rewired, tested, and nutted down. Chrome parts reappeared in white crinkly tissue wrappers, and started to go back on the car. Everything was coming along just fine.

I should mention, in the light of the unexpected major work we were doing on the Auburn, that I had received a letter from the previous owner shortly after we had made the trade, advising that the '52 Mercedes had lost her oil on the trip back to Atlanta, and required an engine overhaul. How come, we asked ourselves, did we drive it almost 400 miles with no trouble? Had they pushed it too hard? Thinking too of the tremendous work we had been forced to do on the Auburn, it was best to believe that we had both acted in good faith. But his letter still rankled a little.

The matter of the dented fender was next on the strategy list. We were coming close to the end of the various scratched-out sheets, and it was early October, still three weeks to the meet. We agreed that if we could find a painter, we'd have it done professionally, except that we dreaded taking the car in its magnificent condition to a shop where it would undoubtedly be pushed about, covered with sandpaper dust, and even possibly damaged. Up until then, we had avoided doing any paint work on our own, but after this discussion, Arthur pulled another rattling surprise out of his compressor. "I think it's time we showed the so-called pros how paint work should be done!" he vowed. This was a new facet in his capability index-rating, and though proposed without fanfare, I already knew he wouldn't make the recommendation without a pretty good certainty that we would succeed. He assured me that with our combined concentration and effort we could do a better job than anyone available. This new personal area of restoration work intrigued me, and we got on with the job immediately.

Arthur was a good teacher. I learned to file, strip, and fill. He showed me the uses of fiberglass, aluminum putty, final filler materials, and all the tricks of using wet-and-dry sandpapers from number 120 to number 600. He produced a big paint sprayer outfit (I was no longer surprised at anything he did) and played it like a virtuoso. We matched the color identically by driving the car over to the paint supply house and having the formulation made up on the spot.

When completed, there was only one small surprise that was also an unexpected bonus. The newly finished fender was slightly better than the rest of the car.

POSTSCRIPTS BY MY WIFE
Alan says that he had decided he would never let me drive the playful Excalibur. Who asked him? That charged-up salamander gave me the willies. Just to look at her was enough for me to shy away. That sporty I'm not! I guess she must have sensed my wary mistrust—why else did she try to dump me and my boy out of her lap on that bumpy street? Glad to see her go, I was.

For different reasons, I never wanted to drive Big Red either. He's all male, and a yard wide. Those big sweeping red torpedo fenders are as bul-

bous as W. C. Fields' nose; that long, arching, arrow-shaped boattail and those menacing chrome exhaust pipes are definitely not for me. "He" always makes me think of a charging red bull, even standing still in the garage. I'm always afraid someday he'll come crashing through into the dining room! But he's a gorgeous hunka' man, can't take that away from Big Red.

With Arthur on a regular Saturday schedule playing restorer with Alan out in the garage, things were somewhat quieter for me. Only now and then did I hear a desperate call for help for me to join the battle. This would happen when they'd finally tear some big parts out of the engine for repair or spraying, and found they couldn't get their big mitts into the tight spots to find a lost nut, or finish a paint area. Then I'd climb up and sit on a fender with my feet in the engine room (good thing I have size six feet) and proceed with the painting, cleaning, and polishing. I went by my cardinal rule: if it moves, clean it. If it's stationary, paint it!

Sí, sí, that was a long hot summer. But we were fairly cool in our semi-air-conditioned garage working lovingly on our big red Tinkertoy.

17

Ready to Win

 The vast, meticulous job on Big Red neared completion by mid-October. All the really heavy work was done, and Arthur had literally found a home *under* the car. Little notes left for me on the family room TV set kept asking for more big nuts, bolts, and screws. I brought them home like candy, in ten-pound box assortments, and they all disappeared into the undercarriage like bonbons into the circus fat lady. All in all, we estimate that the Auburn devoured about 100 pounds of sheet metal carmel creams, chocolate covered nuts, lemon-flavored bolts, and chewy nougat fasteners. We could never understand, in retrospect, why she hadn't fallen apart like an old barnyard flivver on the wedding trip down from North Florida.

With almost two weeks still available for the patiently waiting Rolls, we sensed that she had contemptuously and haughtily ignored the primping of her red-bodied colleague alongside that had gone on all summer.

"I've had all that," she seemed to sniff in her elegant grandeur, "you neophytes are really a ghastly bore!" Despite these exasperating attitudes, we knew she was damned pleased to see us turn our full attentions to her cosmetics counter.

One of her constant plagues that we were determined to cure was the undependable vacuum tank system. We had guessed correctly that part of the carburetor problem must be the leaky and weak vacuum, which acts much the same as a fuel pump in newer cars. It was therefore resolved that we would pull out the whole package, perform major surgery, cad-plate the moving parts, rebuild as needed, and put an end forever to the wheezing and gasping that kept tormenting us.

An unheralded mass of parts astonishingly flowed out of the half-gallon reservoir tank. All sorts of springs, latches, lifters, valves, connectors, and linkages were conjured out of that top-hat shaped vessel. Years of rust scales and grainy, fine coffee-grinds were scooped out of the bowl, an illuminating indication of where the troubles lay. Some of the parts were bent and scarred, others were weakened from years of pumping away with no repair or surcease. Some small parts had to be remade, others cleaned up, straightened out, and replated. Three sleek-as-a-seal coats of black sprayed-on-enamel, prior to reinstallation, was the final coup de grâce to any gremlins still lurking in the crevices of the gasoline fuel system.

For beauty's sake, we copper-plated the cover, cad-plated the exposed valves, and polished the brass and copper lines that fed in and out of the vacuum tank. All this was verified as authentic from pictures and descriptions in various Rolls Royce manuals. There wasn't much else we could find to do on this truly superlative automobile. A few wires here and there were replaced because of slightly frayed ends, and new terminals were silver-soldered to the others. A little engine block wipe-up with lightly tinted liquid aluminum coating, gave Madam Rolly that smooth Cover Girl look.

We were satisfied that she was ready, at last, to take her rightful First Place.

The final big subject on the Auburn board was the check out of the canvas top and whatever improvement we could make to its general fit and installation procedure. We drove Big Red over to our favorite upholstery shop for analysis. The balky top behaved as we expected—it wouldn't lay up easily to the windshield frame, it puckered in the rear, and in careful study, it seemed too small. We realized it had shrunk, but as it was quite new and in excellent cosmetic condition, it was hard to understand how this could have occurred. My inclination was to tear it off and have a new one made. Would that I had followed that hunch—what annoyance we would have saved ourselves in the ensuing week.

By forcing and straining, however, we were finally able to clamp it down, and George agreed that it would be a shame to scrap it. Instead, he said we would move the dot fasteners and the snap-ons about half an inch and thus loosen it up a bit. This seemed logical, and it did help a lot. The next decision was to remove the non-authentic Plexiglas windshield material, and the two panels were replaced with correct safety glass.

Events were to prove shortly why Plexiglas was used.

We brought the car back to George for final fitting of the top. He phoned me a few hours later with bad news. Upon refastening the top, *both* new glass panels had cracked under the stress of the taut top as the wing nuts were being tightened. We cogitated about this clue, and decided to loosen the dot fasteners another half inch. Back she went to the glass shop; two new glass panels were installed. I brought the Auburn home without having tried another clamp-down, feeling that we should guarantee result by first reworking the front wood bow, as suggested by the glass installer. It was his guess that this would relieve the pressure considerably and insure success.

We devoted about half of the final Saturday before the show to this woodworking project. Then we held our breaths and pulled the top onto the windshield frame, gently tightening the wing nuts. Cr-a-a-ack! went the left glass plate. We sighed, and went back to the carpentry alteration, cutting the channel back further on the left side. If it worked on the right panel, we reasoned, it will have to work on the left. At $6 a glass, this wasn't too serious, but it had to be solved! A new glass was made from a template. This time we installed it ourselves, and our final effort to reduce stress proved successful. We then were able to scrub the top energetically on the car with enzymes and detergents. Hosed and sparkling clean, we left it out in the sun for drying, after which it was removed and stowed for use at the show. This procedure proved to be a mistake, as we soon discovered.

As usual, the final preparation week before the show was the standard bash and semi-panic. Arthur took off the entire week, using accumulated sick-leave time privileges. It was hard for us to realize that we had spent five months of weekends and many in-between hours on the fully restored

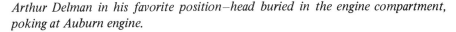

Arthur Delman in his favorite position—head buried in the engine compartment, poking at Auburn engine.

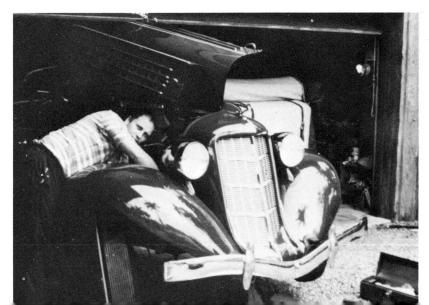

Speedster. True, this was Arthur's first foray into the world of restoration, and, frankly, perhaps he was too meticulous about many aspects of the job. But that's the nature of the man, and it would have done no good to remonstrate with him at any point in the program. He knew the deadline date as well as I did, and that was that. So we plugged on together, sometimes groggily and dispirited.

Our numerous checklists were now well-worn and scratched out, depleted to the point where a fresh "gather up" sheet of final details was prepared. Each day we crossed off a few more items, and by mid-week we were down to the nonessentials. We had also gone over some of the remaining minor details on the Rolls during that final week, and were satisfied that she too was eminently ready for competition. Both cars had been heavily cleaned and waxed during the week by a strong-armed car polisher, brought to my garage for this point-wheedling operation.

Early on Friday morning, we decided to install the newly scrubbed and shiny canvas top, which had been carefully wrapped and stored. Judging required that canvas be "in position" on a car, and we didn't want to chance getting into a grapple-hassle right at the meet. The rear end was snapped on first, and we gently lowered the front bow onto the posts. It simply would not reach! We sadly realized that our scrubbing and sun drying had again shrunk the canvas. We pushed and strained furiously, mindful of the stress on glass. It clearly was not going to fit. Bobbie, Arthur and I stood back aghast at the full meaning of this failure just one day before the show!

After all the months of heart-rending effort, planning and sweat, cash expended, hopes and dreams, could we even consider not being able to take the Speedster to the big show? We knew that not displaying the top installed could be a five-point loser! Resisting this horrid possibility to our toenails, we began to plan a line of attack. First, we soaked the top again with a pressure hose, hoping that it would stretch enough to pull over the clamping studs. This gained about a quarter of an inch barely eked out of the sturdy canvas. Sick with recriminations—"we should have made a new top," etc.—Bobbie and I slumped onto the bench in the garage, holding our heads and moaning. Suddenly, we heard a happy yell from Arthur, our Miracle Worker. We rushed outside and there was the top neatly installed, and no cracked glass in sight. Our invincible and imaginative friend had found a way to put the top on in reverse, clamping the front bow on *first*, and then, by loosening the bolts on the middle brace, gaining about an inch of movement to the rear fasteners. I would never have thought of this in a million years. Hallelujah! We were in business again.

Final test drives were made with both cars. The Auburn went through her paces beautifully, as though determined to give us no more trouble. "Enough is enough," she purred sweetly. We eased her back into her slot in the garage, and started up the Rolls. I drove up the street happily, everything was percolating perfectly. But suddenly the Grande Dame remembered the Chicago trade-off deal, and dropped her tailpipe with a clatter and a crash. Without trying to out-think the old devil—I didn't see what Arthur had seen from down the street; he was already running after me—I made a sharp "U" turn, then backed up gently on the narrow street. I felt the dragging pipe catch a bump in the road, jammed on the brakes too late, and cursed her for outgaming me. I scrambled out of the Rolls just as Arthur came puffing up the hill. He yanked the pipe out from under the car, and we both just stood there dumbly, beating our heads.

The heavy steel tube had kinked at a sixty-degree angle, and cracked right at the bend. Now it looked like the Rolls would not make it to the meet!

There certainly wasn't time on Friday afternoon to have a new pipe bent, we knew that. There was only one solution. Somehow it had to be straightened. We put it in the vise, and started banging away with a small sledgehammer. Except for further denting the bend, it remained adamant. The Rolls stood by smirking silently. "Fix that if you can, you heroes," she seemed to be saying. "That'll teach you!"

I glared at her angrily. "You old biddy," I spat out, "you ought to be on television, 'My Enemy, the Rolls'!"

Characteristically responding to this super-emergency, Arthur decided he'd have to get into his plant that evening where he could heat the tailpipe cherry-red in the big forge, and try to rebend it to shape. We still had some other small items to finish up, so he left this last-ditch effort for later that night. It would either work, or it wouldn't, so there was no point in rushing away at that very moment.

By 10:00 P.M., we polished off the little leftovers, and he marched out with the twisted pipe under his arm, a brave, straight-backed soldier to the end. He waved reassuringly as we dismally watched him drive off. I guess, at that instant, we really couldn't feel or care much anymore. After all the miserable years of the pre-show Friday night, what else could we expect? But we went to bed still hoping, and believing that Arthur would come through as always. At 8:00 A.M. he was back, triumphantly carrying the straightened, welded pipe, freshly blacked with hi-temp paint, a further improvement. As he installed the section under the car, he described his three-hour battle from eleven to 2:00 A.M.

"There I stood at the blast furnace, masked and covered with wet cloths, swinging a sledge hammer like Vulcan in purgatory. Flames leaped about my arms and face. Oh, what a scene. I'll never forget it. I came away black and parched, but with the damn pipe fixed."

What can you do for a friend like that? I hugged him warmly when he crawled out from under the car and stood up. "Hey! Watch out for my blisters!" he yelled happily.

We packed the families into the cars, and took off about 9:30 A.M. We were on our way, and feeling great. What could go wrong now? But the Rolls had not yet discharged her final venom to even the score with me. About ten miles from the show grounds, running at about 60 mph on the expressway, with a clatter and a knocking she "blew" a valve. I rolled off the expressway, vowing to get in touch with the Chicago Duesenberg owner before I was a day older. The Auburn was momentarily lost in traffic somewhere behind me, but it suddenly appeared and Arthur and Bobbie saw me flailing my arms on the roadside. A Volkswagen almost climbed up on the boattail as they veered over and came to a stop a few hundred feet ahead.

Arthur dashed up with his tool box in hand, but I waved him away despairingly. "You and Bobbie go on to the show," I said with finality. "This is just too much, we've had it."

"Nothing doing," said Mister Invincible. "Let's have a look."

Sure enough, he had the answer. When the head cover was removed, he found valve number 5 sticking way up in the air like a big sore thumb. With a whack of the hammer, and a few shots of Marvel oil, he ordered me to start her up. Heart in mouth as always, I hit the starter pedal, and she roared into life, throbbing smoothly as though nothing had ever happened between us. It was then I knew I had been forgiven at last. "I'll behave now," I could almost hear her whisper to me.

Had there been a Hard Luck Trophy at this meet, we would have won it hands down. As it was, *both* cars won First Place in their classes at Pier 66! This was really the greatest tribute to Our Man Who Had a Front Row Seat on Mount Olympus.

POSTSCRIPTS BY MY WIFE

The show at Pier 66 was a good show, a really good show, and not only because we won big, though that helps!

The place was nice; it's always cool and breezy out there. The club people are always courteous and cooperative and friendly, and my picnic lunch stretched as far as was needed and then some. I found a nice shady tree near the Auburn and took up my guard duty while various persons—Arthur, his wife Goldy, his brother, and sometimes Alan—stood guard at the Rolls across the field.

I was just handing someone a cold drink (and nearly dropped it in my pastel lap) as I heard the loud wham of one of the Auburn doors being slammed, followed by the clang of metal on concrete as one of our newly chromed door handles hit the ground. I jumped up in astonishment, just as Alan happened on the scene.

A young woman shamefacedly stood there by the door, half-frozen with shock and remorse. Alan looked at her in disbelief. "Why did you do that, Madame?" he asked quietly, as he stooped to pick up the handle.

"I don't really know" she said in bewilderment. "I guess I just wanted to see if they make cars like they used to!"

Thank God they used to, I breathed to myself. The door was uninjured, and the handle went back easily; the cotter pin had merely fallen out from the impact. We bent it back on itself tightly this time. Good thing too, the judges were leaving the adjacent car and approaching the Auburn just as Alan gave the pin a final twist.

Bless the sight-seers. But someone please tell them to keep their hands off the cars!

18

The End of the Caper

It hasn't been mentioned before for lots of reasons, but mostly because our cars would have heard me, and who knows what they could do to us! Our other love could hardly hope to vie with the ponderous allegiance we have given to our endless Automobile Caper. But, in addition to wheels in our brains, there has always been a coursing stream of salt in our veins.

My first excursion into the sailing life occurred at the age of 17, when unknown to our parents, my closest friend and I pooled our teen-age resources and bought a 16-foot, Comet class, oak-decked sailboat. She was a natural-born capsizer from the word go (or was I?). But I earned my water-wings in her, and she whetted my appetite for more. Some years later I graduated to a 23-foot cabin sloop named "Hideaway." This embellished my bachelor years, and tied in nicely with the glossy early Detroit Iron. Through the years I sailed and crewed on various hulls from 6-to-85-footers. I can honestly say, with the exception of the four war years (when I even managed to grab a sail in Guam or Manila) that I have always owned a sailboat of one sort or another, right up to the present.

Barbara too has a touch of the "Auld Salt" in her, as her father, at the age of 18, was a channel pilot in the St. Lawrence, and a sometimes-Captain, with papers, in the years before he lighted into the automobile field. Actually though, she is really a pretty timid sailor technically. But I forgive her the snarled lines and goosewinged spinnakers, because she loves the wind in her face and can sleep as blissfully as a child stretched out on deck, fully secure in the knowledge that I'm at the helm. Better there, she says, than in the Rolls!

Our only problem has been to try to find the time to sail! Most Saturdays are given wholesale to the cars, as we wistfully glance out to the dock where our 25-foot fiberglass sloop bobs up and down in the breeze, within arm's reach. We look at her again, shake our heads, and then resolutely head for the fumey garage. But now and then, we do manage to break this viselike grip and sail away for a day. We have necessarily conjured up an interesting rationale that goes something like this: "Now that we live right on the Bay looking at water all the time, why do we have to sail?" Such logic! But it helps.

To free ourselves completely, we might have to part with the cars (except for the Rolls; she'd hound us). That idea makes us mildly apoplectic. Money alone could never balance the ledger of personal commitment we have given to our wonderful automobiles.

In the meantime, we hurry to the battle call, primping our cars for bigger and, we hope, better competition. Do automobiles create sex drives? I wonder. I'll have to check my dusty old Psych textbooks.

Sometimes we feel we've had enough of the cars as a dominating way of life. What we really mean, I guess, is that we've had enough of the show world—it begins to drag at the human spirit to have to whip the cars into shape a half-dozen times a year. We've had enough of the kicks, aggravations, rewards, disappointments, emoluments, and gratifications. And I haven't a bit of space left in my den for another trophy, show plaque, or picture. We also know deep down that we'll never stop looking at vintage car publications or the "For Sale" ads, or avoid automatically craning our necks every time we pass an auto junk yard on a country road, or an open barn door in a meadow. Every great Classic car will be a potential trap for us as long as we live. Yes, we know that. Those are deeply built-in reflexes, and the lure of a possible prize-winner flares our nostrils, and we bay like hounds in a fox hunt. We fight to control these terrible urges.

And yet . . . and yet. There's still that beautiful, almost-restored Duesenberg LeBaron convertible sedan in Chicago!

If there's an Everest left to climb in the rigorous antique car world, that's the one for us. After that, we solemnly tell each other, there would be no need to climb anymore. We've owned, and loved, and shown some of the greatest vintage cars ever built, and not to have a Duesey, we admit, would be like collapsing in a heap just before the finish-line string, with a 3:58 mile behind us!

We're now trying to figure out how big a motorsailer we would need to carry a 2 1/2 ton, nineteen-foot car on the foredeck.

POSTSCRIPTS BY MY WIFE

Now that we've come to the finale of this bittersweet chronicle, we wouldn't want you to think that owning these great cars and living under their dominating iron rule is an indication that it's all trouble. No Sir-eee!

Besides the exciting and colorful car shows and special events, just driving them around to keep their circulation up can be great fun and a rich source of pride. On Sundays we usually throw open our garage doors and take our pick of the harem lovelies awaiting our pleasure. The neighbors always watch as we go by—they never know which one it will be. They wave as we drive by, and I think they're secretly pleased to have us down at the bottom of the little peninsula. (I surmise this by the way we meet strangers here and there who say, "Oh, you're the people who live down at the bottom of Poinciana with all the old cars." And then they usually mention the name of one or the other of our neighboring families.)

One neighbor surprised us one September by bringing home a 1935 Bentley drophead coupe from Europe. After years of wandering over on Saturdays and watching us enviously, the bug had finally bitten him. The big mistake he made was being too proud to ask our advice—which we'd have gladly given. Without the knowledge it takes to restore a car, he stumbled around looking for the answers. His unhappy car, a rather blunt, stodgy model, ended up sitting on blocks in his carport for many months, swept by salt mists and wind from the bay until the old paint started flaking off in globs. Then the car suddenly disappeared, and we learned it had gone to a paint shop. The evil eye was surely on her then, we knew that! About six months later, upon our inquiry, he admitted that the painters had driven him daffy. He finally sold it in its unfinished state. Goodbye to that local competition.

Our little village of Coconut Grove is very "arty" and has lots of charming little Stratford-on-Avon kinds of shops, and a lovely theatrical Playhouse. There are mansard roofs, mullioned windows, and replica sidewalk gas lamps among the leafy trees. The young people (you may call them hippies if you wish) congregate here on weekends in their long saintly hair styles and way-out clothes. As we drive through the center in the Rolls, they stop on the sidewalks, hand raised in the peace sign, calling happily, "Oh, beautiful man!" and "Hey, far out—cool!" Obviously there's no generation gap in things of classic beauty.

Everyone loves the old cars. . . .

Epilogue

So You Thought That Was the End of the Cars?

So did we, really!

We went to Europe for most of the summer of 1971, with no specific purpose in mind except to have fun and give Bennett "the tour." We mainly intended to visit a bit in France, then along the Mediterranean and middle Italy. We promised each other faithfully that we would bypass the vintage car circuit while in England.

With this straight-faced, practical, and sober decision, sealed by a firm handshake, we arrived in London in late June. After a morning of recovering from the time-change of the trip, and an afternoon of window-shopping, our mutual treaty of solidarity began to melt down like drippings on a hot candle. After some tentative hemming and hawing, British style, we broke down just a little.

"Pity to be in London, and not say hello to Jack!" So we sailed over in a taxi, "just for the fun of it," to visit Jack Bond at Vintage Autos, Ltd.

Luck was on our side this time. Jack had *nothing* on the floor that would have worried us in our sleep, even without the modicum of resistance we had built in beforehand. We spent a pleasant hour with our old friend, invited him to come over to Florida and stay with us for the 1971 AACA show in October. We took off, relieved that no terrible temptation had been waiting to pounce on us in the dark crannies of Brooks Mews.

Then the old alumnae spirit caught us, but good. Just the sight of those beautiful old cars at Jack's was enough to set the glands flowing. We headed right over to Frank Dale, Ltd. (and Stepsons), a favorite place for Americans looking for Rolls and Bentley Classics. Like Harry's American Bar, it's where you had to go to get the feel of things in London's car trade. We no longer looked at each other apologetically, the fun was on! We were skating on our favorite thin ice, the music was playing a waltz, and I had my best girl by the hand and my young skater, Bennett, on the other side. Who could ask for anything more?

We stepped out of the taxi right at the courtyard entrance of Dale's, and were greeted smack across the eyes by the *one* automobile that should *never* have been there. Not sporting fair and square! There stretched one of the rarest of its breed, a glistening white 1956 S-1 Bentley Continental convertible.

I whistled through my sigh, and glanced furtively at Bobbie. She shaded her eyes with her hands, as though hoping to avoid the confrontation. Here we were, touching again on a cornerstone in our relationship, the ability to flex out of a given posture as circumstances demanded, into a total reversal on a moment's notice. This ability for change-of-mind is a wellspring of our camaraderie. It works in both directions, allowing of course for the stronger male stubborness, in proper proportion.

My organized wife wasn't quite ready to give up so fast. In an impulsive moment of confidence she once gave me a clue; that her "challenging attitude" is a testing scale, where she can weigh my level of certainty on any given subject. Wise girl. So I knew that she intended to pique me into some needling self-analysis, balancing my knowledge of this car and my judgment about its rarity and value. There was a selling job to be done—I definitely *knew* I wanted this great Bentley! Part of my apologia was already building in my mind as we started our inspection of the handsome piece.

There was no doubt about it. The unique and characteristic tail-fin on the rear fender, with its cluster of vertical triple lights molded into the back edge, caught her fancy at once. Without knowing anything about this rare car, she had spotted the outstanding elements that clearly separated the Continental from the standard S-1 model. I began my campaign to win her over, knowing that my certainty was so strong that she would succumb agreeably as our little charade progressed. It was all set in my private fourth dimension; I had sparkling visions of driving around Europe in this masterpiece. The idea of touring the Continent in a Continental (what else was it for?) suited me just fine, and made me nostalgic for the places of Henry James and Scott Fitzgerald. Ah, that was a world I had missed, but it wasn't too late. I could do it in my 1956 Classic.

The lovely Bentley S-1 Continental Convertible.

It was easy to see out of the side of my eye that Bobbie was excited, and getting more and more involved. The salesman did a nice low-pressure job of it; that helped. He undid the boot and raised the top, fastened the clamps easily, and showed us the neatly tailored headliner. He laid the top back again, and ran his hands tenderly over the rich, plush red leather. Bobbie then expertly checked out the chrome and the paint, all newly restored, and I could see that she was having a hard time finding fault. The time had come, I said to myself, to talk of many things, of cabbages and kings. I asked the price, and was a bit shocked at the figure. The British are finally getting wise to us Yanks, I reflected, and it's about time. We've been abducting their loveliest Classic cars across the ocean for years. They might as well get paid for the sacrifice. Even vintage wines had gone up in price.

I decided not to dicker on the price, having other ideas of what was needed. But first I had to find out if the car could be made ready for a Saturday afternoon departure. It was already Tuesday, and I wouldn't make a formal decision until the following morning anyway. Then there was the matter of having the funds transferred from my bank in Miami to Barclay's in London. Pretty short notice, but the eager salesman assured us it could be done. I gave him a list of the items I wanted completed in three days, and he whistled worriedly at the extent of my requirements. I would pay their price, but wanted everything to be first rate; new tires, brakes, electrical, a major tune-up, leather softening, paint touch-ups, and polish: the works.

He politely suggested we stop back after lunch; he would need a conference with his boss. We strolled down the street to a little woody Italian restaurant. I took the opportunity to get in my first licks. Bennett was shaking with excitement, I knew whose side *he* was on. I had warned him before we left Dale's not to bollux up the deal, and good politician that he is, he kept his mouth shut. He knew his Daddy, and he knew his Mommy, and he had a fair idea of how we'd come out! Good kid. My buddy. I'd exploit him only if *absolutely* last-ditch tactics were demanded. My first and most delectable sales pitch, was, of course, the "use all summer of this magnificent car all over Europe." We had planned to rent a Mercedes the second week out in Belgium anyway, I pointed out, so why blow all that rental money for a couple of months, when we could apply it to the cost of the Bentley?

These combined lines of economic facts were very strong field goals against a mild wind. It almost finished the job, right then and there. Bobbie almost *had* to agree; it was pure logic. She then demanded to know what I would do with the car back home—did I *really* think I'd use it for everyday purposes, right-hand drive and all? I answered yes, my most sincere Madison Avenue look on my face. She arched her eyebrows and said nothing. That was a good sign. I quickly changed the subject to the eggplant parmigiano.

After lunch, we wandered out to look in the window of a funny little antique shop that was really not an antique shop, but more of a curio collection. The little store was filled to the brim with hand-carved wooden statues, gateposts, ships' prowheads, brass eagles, a wooden lion and a full size ebony Nubian statue. There was also a hand-carved wooden baby elephant standing about waist high, a stone head of a bull, and assorted wood pub-sign carvings hung around the walls. One group of heavy wooden paintings caught my eye, and held me captivated. Apparently, they were paintings of Henry the Eighth's wives, but there were only three—where were the other three? The shopowner admitted rather shamefacedly that he needed money and had recently divided the set. I almost cried. What a pity! However, the "best" three wives were left, Katharine of Aragon, Anne Boleyn, and Jane Seymour, the most celebrated. Why had the other joker taken the other three? Probably because they were in better physical condition, I surmised. Anyway, I mentally added these huge castle-wall objets d'art to my Bentley campaign.

She wouldn't have believed me anyway, if I told her we were going to buy them and try to stuff them in the trunk of the Bentley for transport to

Antwerp (the main European port of exit for ships to Miami). Why worry her with details, one thing at a time, old boy.

Dale's accepted my terms and the rush, three-day delivery. Under gentle pressure that evening but not enough to nurture a future "I told you so" from my wife, our pro-and-con conference on the subject ended amicably. Fact is, I always enjoy a car more when Bobbie has shown wholehearted desire to have it too. That's only good diplomacy, and takes the "rub" out in case anything goes wrong later. Then I can blame her.

Arrangements were consummated the following morning, and we were able to proceed with the London tourist itinerary we had long promised Bennett. We rented a small British car from Avis, were blessed by a dented rear fender during the day while parked for shopping, saw the precision changing of the Guard at Buckingham Palace, took the smelly boat ride down the industrial Thames, visited Big Ben (small Ben *had* to see this landmark!), went to the movies in Piccadilly Circus, and wound up the whirlwind day with fish and chips, around the corner from Trafalgar Square. And, oh yes, we rode nowhere in particular on the upper level of a red double decker London bus.

On Friday, I announced that I wanted to run over to Dale's to see how they were coming along. As I was leaving, I mentioned casually to Bobbie, one foot out the door, that "I would be picking up the paintings at the same time."

She looked at me levelly. "Why take them today? We can stop by tomorrow and load them right into the car on the way out." What a cool customer.

And that's what we did. Except that we did not get out on Saturday, though the Bentley was ready as promised. On Friday I had learned at Dale's

The Bentley Continental on the quay at Saint Tropez.

that the annual Bentley Concours d'Elegance was to be held in Kensington Gardens (Hyde Park) the following afternoon. We certainly weren't about to miss this unexpected dividend. Proudly we drove up to the gate in our prancing white knight, and were waved through with a flourish. Although we weren't registered for the show, we parked in an immediate roped-off, adjacent area, while the show visitors walked many blocks from parking slots in the surrounding streets. The Bentley had been our ticket of admission.

It was a fantastic show—that's the only word for it. Hundreds of the world's greatest Bentleys from 1920 on stood cheek-to-cheek along the tree-lined path. There was too much to absorb, and even too much to describe. One vexing disappointment marred the day: a roll of 36-exposure color film, had, without my sensing it, jammed in the starting sprockets, and though I ran about gleefully shooting lurid pictures of the Bentleys, standing on benches, climbing statues, kneeling on my knees, and once even taking a shot upside down, it was all useless—I hadn't turned one single frame! Goodbye to all those goodies: the mahogany boattails, the sleek all-aluminum racers, the side-mount phaetons, the Red Labels, the Blue Labels, the 3 liters, the 4-1/2 liters, the 6-1/2 liters, the fabulous 8 liters; the James Youngs, the Van den Plas, the Gurney-Nuttings, the Park Wards, the Freestone & Webbs, the Franays. All gone and lost forever. Well, maybe not forever, but anyway until another June visit to London.

We took off on Sunday, via Dover on the Channel Ferry to Ostend, Belgium. Two of the huge wooden paintings filled the trunk to the lid. The other was squeezed into the back seat space with all the luggage, and Bennett sat uncomfortably on a pillow between the bucket seats in front. What a fuss over the Bentley on the boat. With a Sunday boatload of tourists and local transients returning from a big weekend in England, we must have looked like the Duke and Duchess of Coc-nut County. Sans monocle, of course.

We slowly made our way through France to the Riviera and then on into Italy via San Remo.

We shot pictures of the milk-white Bentley backgrounded by the deep blue Mediterranean Sea. Wherever we went, we drew a small curious crowd— there had only been 14 of these convertible Continentals produced in a three-year period. Except for the fact that the Bentley felt like a battleship surrounded by darting Renault and Fiat torpedo boats throughout the tour, and my getting jammed tightly more than once in the narrow streets of quaint French and Italian towns, she behaved like a dream all the way. At 90 mph, we felt like we were sitting in our living room lounge chairs.

In Florence, we yielded to a full set of new brown leather luggage, Italian style, with red, white, and green canvas stripes running around like a belt. When we discarded our old worn luggage in the hotel room, the porters came running after us, gesticulating wildly and yelling in Italian that we had for-gotten our bags. I stopped and finally made them understand that they could keep them with our blessings. They stared at us dumbfounded as we drove off.

In Bologna, Italy, we made a pilgrimage to the Lamborghini factory, took the tour, snapped pictures of Bennett sitting proudly at the wheel of a bright mustard-colored Miura, and finished up by eating canelloni and veal scallo-pine in the old city piazza, while comparing the leaning tower there to the one Bobbie and Bennett climbed to the top of in Pisa while I waited out of breath halfway up the crazy tilted staircase.

The wondrous Bentley is home now, under the canopy tent on the left side of the house. She is none the worse for wear after the sea voyage from Savona, Italy, to Jacksonville, Florida, and the final drive down to Miami. Arthur and I have naturally found "some things that need attending to," in our own inimitable fashion, to make her a showpiece.

You'll have to excuse me now. I have to rush out to pick up a big box of Bentley chrome parts at the platers, and a new set of sparkplugs.

By the way, I'll be driving the Buick.

Home at last. The Bentley joins the family of cars in front of the author's house, with the Auburn, Rolls, and Aston-Martin forming the welcoming party.

Publisher's Note

As this book was being prepared for press, the 1936 Auburn Boattail Speedster won the long sought-after, elusive, National AACA First Prize—a fitting tribute to ten years of arduous effort by the author and his wife, and a well-deserved reward at the big meet at Fort Lauderdale in April 1972.

The Radcliff boys, Bennett and Jonathan, polishing the Auburn Boattail Speedster the day before the big win in Fort Lauderdale.